Bend Over Shake A Tailfeather!

To Clint
Merry
Christmas

BILL PRIVETTE

Bill Privette

Photography and art are by the author unless otherwise attributed.

Published by Tailfeather Press & Taxidermy International, 1119 Hendricks Avenue, Jacksonville, NC 28540.
www.turkeyhuntbooks.com

ISBN 0-9777229-0-2
First printing, unabridged, November 2005
Second printing, abridged, January 2006

Library of Congress Control Number
2005910997
Privette, Bill
Bend Over Shake A Tailfeather!
Tall tales, gibberish & malarkey while hunting wild turkeys.
Second Edition.
1. Turkey Hunting – anecdotes, facetiae, satire
2. Outdoor Life – anecdotes, facetiae, satire

Printed in the United States by Morris Publishing
3212 East Highway 30
Kearney, NE 68847
1-800-650-7888

CONTENTS

The author with fall gobbler at Rose Brook farm in Missouri. For over the past 30 years, Bill has written and edited for various publications: *The Dayton (Ohio) Daily News, Barron's Outdoor Guide, Outdoor Life, Sports Afield, Fly Fisherman, Turkey Hunter, Wildlife in North Carolina, Fur-Fish-Game* and dozens more. His photography has won national awards. His newsletter, *Tailfeathers*, has entertained friends all over the country. He is a gifted public speaker and is available to speak at events and banquets. He is an active NWTF member. Contact him at 1119 Hendricks Ave., Jacksonville, NC 28540. Phone: 910.455.5713. Photo by Jeff Bierman, DMD.

FOREWORD & GRATUITY

"For everything there is a season and a time for every matter under heaven...a time to seek and a time to lose; a time to keep and a time to cast away." *Ecclesiastes.*

And I would add a time to hunt turkeys and a time to wait. A time to write a book or two at last. There was a time in my life when I did not hunt turkeys. I hunted other winged creatures with the religious fervor of a new convert. I grew up in the South, hunting quail with bird dogs, shooting doves while standing in a picked cornfield, traipsing through the mountain brush for ruffed grouse and sitting in a duck boat or blind, freezing my butt off. When I moved to the Midwest I converted to pheasant hunting. It was worth the effort, most of the time. In other words, I shot a lot of pheasants.

I told myself that I would never live happily in a place that did not offer pheasant hunting. That was before I shot my first wild turkey. The last day of the 1988 Ohio spring season in Vinton County. It took me three years of screw-ups to accomplish this feat. But it was worth every minute of trying.

Some people can remember their first love, their first beer, their first whatever and how it changed their lives. I remember my first turkey hunt as if it were yesterday. Naturally, the tornado helps the memory. My life has never been the same. I have chased wild turkeys for over 20 years and I have come to realize that nothing stays the same. Even the best turkey hunting situations will come and go. It is the wise person who takes advantage of his blessings while he has them, knowing that all things are transitory – health, friends, family, good hunting ground, life itself.

I have been incredibly fortuitous to have hunted wild turkeys with lots of great friends in lots of different and wonderful places all over the country. Some of those friends are gone now. Some have moved away. Some have died. Many of the places are gone now, too. The farms have been sold. The land has been developed. Parking lots, malls and housing developments reside in much of my old territory. New hunt clubs arrive with new leases and new members with deeper pockets. Nothing really remains the same forever.

This book is dedicated to all my hunting buddies, past and present. You know who you are because many of you will be revealed in this book and other books later. Your friendships are special gifts and I cherish them each day. Your companionship in the quest of wild game, small and large, feathered and furred, but especially in the pursuit of that pinnacle of panache, that mountain top of tremendous, that brassy bird of bodaciousness, the wild turkey, has meant more to me than I can express in words. Lies maybe, gibberish, perhaps, balderdash, certainly, but words, no.

May we hunt turkeys until the day we die. And then some more.

Gobble, gobble. ↓↓

The author poses with 26-pound gobbler shot at Rose Brook Farm in Missouri. He was still short of tooth and long of breath in those days. Photo by Jeff Bierman, DMD.

CHAPTER ONE

"Turkey Hunting Saved My Life"
Hunting Turkeys for the First Time

After significant consideration, cogitation and contemplation, I have determined that I am a sign person. No, I do not mean sign language - talking with fingers. I can do that but I have a very limited vocabulary – point, come here, middle finger, death ray, hook-em horns, OK, thumb's up. That's about it. What I mean is I SEE and interpret signs. Omens. Portents. Auguries. Stuff like that.

For example, after freezing my butt off all morning in a duck boat in Wayne County, Ohio, one duck, the only duck in the state of Ohio, flies by at nose bleed altitude on its way to Kentucky. I mutter to myself, "Forsooth! A sign." The little voice inside my head says, "Sell the darn duck boat and decoys and start turkey hunting." I did.

In retrospect, it's a good thing, too. The way I hunted ducks in those early days, the risks I took and the crazy stunts I managed to survive, if I had not switched to turkey hunting, I would be long dead by now. There's a sign for you. It's called a tombstone. Alas, I can say with a certain amount of earnest that turkey hunting saved my life.

"Yes, Dear, but I really need to go turkey hunting. After all it saved my life." Works every time.

Anyway, that was my last duck hunt in Ohio and for many years after that. The very next spring I headed to Vinton County in southeastern Ohio in search of my first wild turkey. Back in those days, the hunting season was short, only a week or so. It was a miracle that anyone actually shot a turkey in those early days. Back then, you had to mail an application to Columbus and get your name drawn for a permit in order to hunt. I did. Next, you had to have a place to go. I did. Finally, you had to know what the heck you were doing. Alas, I did not.

Again, you only had a week or so to do it. A week - or portion thereof due to having to work full-time - is not enough time for rookies to do much except screw up. Needless to say, the success rate was low during the early years for Ohio turkey hunters. And I did every thing in my power to keep the failure rate high.

I remember writing in the Dayton Daily News – the newspaper which featured my weekly outdoor column and articles in the Sunday sports section - that according to ODNR records only 1 out of 7 Buckeye turkey hunters actually killed a turkey. Anyway, rumor has it that Ohio turkey hunters, all 200 more or less, celebrated when I moved to Illinois. They missed my Sunday columns but the state success rate went up the very next year. It was a fair trade off.

However, I must admit that I found it irritating to read the Springfield outdoor writer's articles that featured his lack of success when turkey hunting. I used to feel sorry for him but now I suspect he was brain dead. And no, I did not help him shoot a darn turkey. The guy was on his own. Or better yet, he needed to quit.

At any rate, since I had received a sign, loud and clear. Who was I to ignore it? You ignore signs and you usually pay a price. I sold the duck boat, decoys, the whole kit and caboodle to Uncle Doug, my wife's brother-in-law. It was an easy sell. Big Doug enjoyed sitting in a duck boat while freezing his butt off and watching empty skies. After all, I taught him how to do it.

We used the proceeds from the duck stuff to help buy a beat-up excuse for a Jeep CJ 5 for our oldest son. It was a fixer-upper of the first magnitude. It had more rust than metal and an engine that burned more oil than gas. And I began to study up on turkey hunting. Which did not take very long. And when we were not working on the Jeep.

"Dad, the thing-of-bob doesn't work anymore. Where's the Chilton manual?"

Books were scarce, few and far between, back then and not very helpful. There were no Chilton manuals that broke everything down and showed you how to hunt turkeys bumper to bumper. I managed to find and listen to a rudimentary calling tape or was it a 45 rpm record? Not much help there. TV shows and videotapes were figments of Rob Keck's and Bill Jordan's imagination.

I did attend an ODNR seminar on turkey hunting. The presenter was boring. I am being kind here since I have forgotten his name and do not want to lose a book sale. He was not the sharpest knife in the cutlery department and it became obvious that his expertise was limited to the same book I had read and the same tape I had listened to. So I left with the gut feeling I was basically on my own.

I did know, however, where wild turkeys were to be found. I had discovered them by accident while hunting grouse. Actually, Old Bud, my long departed faithful Gordon setter, found them. What a point! We had been hunting grouse all day and then. Whammo! All of a sudden, he locked up tight, muscles shivering, tail in the air. It was a heck of a point. I tiptoed past him, gun raised, expecting a grouse to explode from the cover. Instead, a 20-pound gobbler blasted up and nearly knocked me down.

Old Bud turned and looked at me. Holy Cow, what the Sam Hill was that? That was my first close encounter with a wild turkey. I had seen them a time or two, while growing up and hunting grouse. But we had no turkey season in those days. And it was rare to even see or hear a turkey in the woods.

Forsooth, I knew where turkeys were to be found. The night before opening day, I left Dayton and drove southeast two-and-a-half hours to Vinton County. To a place called Raccoon State Forest, which was owned by the Mead Paper Company. It was open to public hunting, semi-mountainous, hardwoods, deep creeks, steep hollows and it held wild turkeys.

I got to McArthur around supper time, picked up some burgers at the local McDonald's knock off – McDougal's, with the green arches and no where near a million burgers sold. I drove up into the forest and parked at an old cemetery.

Since I was brand new to turkey hunting, I had no idea how to roost a turkey, hoot like an owl or tell a wing beat from a wing ding. So I sat on the tailgate, ate my supper, drank a brewsky, watered the plants and crawled into bed in the back of my pickup camper shell. And I tried to go to sleep. It was easier to fall asleep when I was a kid on Christmas Eve. The little voice in my head whispered, "Hey, so far, so good. You could be duck hunting in Wayne County, 15 degrees below zero, sitting there all day and not a duck in the sky."

What is it about alarm clocks any way? No matter how tired I am, how much sleep I get or do not get, I always wake up five minutes before the dad blasted thing goes off. Which I did that morning and have ever since. I crawled out of the sleeping bag and the back of the truck and watered the plants again. I sat on the tailgate in my gym shorts and t-shirt and drank hot coffee from my thermos. You can't do that when you are duck hunting. It's too darn cold and the coffee chills quickly. Spring mornings in Ohio can be frosty, but nothing compared to subzero winter duck hunts.

At that moment, I was beginning to like turkey hunting and I had not even left the truck. I pulled on my camo gear, a set of Army surplus woodland BDUs given to me by a retired Green Beret buddy. If Jim Crumley had invented Trebark by then it had not reached the stores in Ohio. I laced up my boots and unzipped my old Winchester 1200 pump, wrapped in special order camo tape. I closed up the truck and slipped into the dark woods with plenty of time to find a spot and sit down while it was still dark.

The flashlight from my toolbox lit the way as I maneuvered through the woods. The going was easy at first and then. *Whack!* An unseen limb slapped me in the face and the stinging pain brought tears to my eyes. As I stood there in agony, the whippoorwills cranked up and whipped their annoying heads off. At least their cacophony camouflaged my sorry attempt to sneak quietly down the hill into the creek bottom.

It did not occur to me at the time that I could be walking right into a roost of turkeys. I was a rookie and had no idea the risk I was taking walking into the turkey woods without the slightest idea of where the turkeys were. Luckily, I did not bump any birds and reached a spot where I figured I would sit and wait.

I had a Lynch box call and had practiced tree yelps with the calling tape, but I was too scared to use it lest I blow the whole deal before it got started. I sat quietly, contented, halfway warm, half-asleep. The little voice reminded me I could be freezing my butt off in ice cold water waiting for ducks to show up when there were no ducks. I waited some more. So far, so good.

The sky lightened up, the whippoorwills shut up and the songbirds woke up. They proceeded to fill the forest with their customary cheery chatter – robins, cardinals, redwing blackbirds and more. It was, after all, mating season in the forest and the birds were optimistic, horny and had a much better chance of scoring than one out of seven. Their cheerful calls were a natural act of males whistling at females, if you think about it.

Heck, I have whistled at my share of babes in my younger years, when I was short of tooth, long of breath and the sap was rising. I started to settle in, relax and reminisce about an early girlfriend, what's-her-name, the sap rising and the drive-in movies, when IT happened. My first gobble. A good one, loud and hearty, from a turkey, roosted in a tree about 75 yards away. I was dazzled. Awe struck. The tiny hairs on the back of my neck stood up. My heart beat faster. Jackpot! The memory of lost love and rising sap evaporated.

It was not until a year later, that I realized just how darn lucky I had been that morning when I sat down when I did. If I had continued on in the dark for another minute or two, I would have walked right into that turkey and bumped it right out of the tree. And, worst of all, I would not have known what the heck I had done.

I was a green rookie that morning, a shade between Day Glo chartreuse and florescent viridian. I almost glowed in the dark. I would learn how to bump birds out of trees my second season of turkey hunting, with the help of Hermit Dave, when we encountered the dreaded Heartbreaker – the smartest, fastest, sneakiest and meanest gobbler that ever lived. Another story, another time.

Tom Kelly says that Ronnie "Cuz" Strickland says that there are no turkey hunting experts, only good amateurs. It did not take me long to become a good amateur at bumping turkeys out of trees.

The bird gobbled again. And again. And I was converted, transported, addicted and hooked. Three gobbles was all it took. You see, not all omens are visual. Some are auditory. The little voice whispered, "There you go, pal. Told you so. And if you play your cards right that guy might even fly down and come to you." Boy was that little voice stupid.

The turkey gobbled on the roost and I finally mustered enough courage to slip my Lynch box call out and crank a couple of soft yelps. To which the gobbler hammered back more gobbles. And I cranked a few more yelps. And the gobbler hammered more gobbles. How about that? I was turkey calling. Piece of cake. Sliced thick, ready to eat and plenty more to go around. Preston Pittman eat your heart out.

The turkey and I conversed for quite a while. But all I knew how to do was yelp. No purrs, clucks, cuts or fancy talk. Just boring yelps. And too many of them. Finally, I thought I heard what sounded like a turkey flying down. Since I had never heard one fly down before, I was just guessing. It would take a couple years of listening and watching turkeys up close before I got the hang of recognizing wing beats.

And there was the time I roosted a ruffed grouse and thought it was a turkey. That was the time Hermit Dave and I were hunting "virgin turkeys" in Athens County. Boy did I feel stupid the next morning when the grouse flew down and almost landed in my lap. The full story is featured later in this book.

More gobbles proceeded from the bird on the ground. I yelped some more. I was getting good at the yelps by now, feeling more confident. More gobbles answered from across the creek bottom. I finally figured it was time to shut up, get my gun up and wait for the bird to come in. That is what the book said to do. The moment of truth, the day of destiny, the showdown. And I commenced to do so. And I wondered if the turkey had read the book and knew what to do, too.

I focused on the direction of the last gobble and scanned the woods for movement. But, before I could see anything, lo and behold, I heard a low rumble in the distance. What the heck? Thunder? Was that thunder? The sky began to darken. The wind picked up. Then flashes of lightning and more thunder. Closer now. And more gobbles. My first shock gobbles when a tom gobbles at loud noises. And the wind really picked up. Next came hail. As big as marbles, whacking me on the legs and head. Not fun.

Within minutes, a perfectly beautiful morning with the promise of a tom coming to the gun had turned into an ugly thunderstorm, complete with earth-shaking thunder, scare-the-crap-out-of-you lightning and wind, lots of wind. Did I mention I am not very fond of lightning? As the storm arrived and the ominous dark clouds swirled overhead, the trees twisted and turned. I forgot all about the turkey across the creek bottom.

Instead I got my butt up fast and headed for the nearest ditch for cover. Needless to say, I left my shotgun behind on the ground lest it conduct a lightning bolt while I held it. I hunkered down in that ditch, praying for salvation. I don't remember what I promised God but I promised a lot. I reminded him that I was too young to die and I had quit duck hunting.

An old Andy Griffith record ended with, "I don't know what it was exactly but I think they call it football." At the time, I did not know exactly what it was but later the local radio station called it a tornado. And for about 15 minutes all hell broke loose. Tree limbs flying, treetops snapping, rain pouring down, thunder, lightning, the works. One wet and scared turkey hunter in the ditch. One wet and scared turkey gobbler hunkered down, who the heck knows where?

The little voice whispered, "By the way, did I remember to tell you that turkey season coincides with tornado season?"

The best thing about tornados, if you could say there is anything good about them, is they don't last as long as hurricanes. Which I have experienced on many occasions as well. And they tend to tear up things in their path but leave everything else alone. Fortuitously, I was not in the path. It hit less than a mile north of me. Which is close enough.

After the storm passed, the sky cleared and the sun came out as if no storm had occurred in the first place. Go figure. So I picked myself up and squished my waterlogged body back to my tree and shotgun. I sat down and proceeded to call on my box call. Nothing doing. Box calls squeak when they are wet. And gobblers do not usually respond to squeaks. Squirrels do. And horny songbirds. But not turkeys.

Since my call was wet, my gun was wet and I was wet to the bone, I could not find anything dry enough to dry the box call. I was, as they are wont to say, SOL. I tried to mimic a yelp or two with my voice, but alas, no response. If the gobbler was still around, which I was not sure it was, it was tuned in to Mr. Lynch.

I sat for awhile contemplating my state of affairs and soon realized that I did not like being wet. I still don't. Too many Boy Scout campouts in the rain. And that is why I do not like to hunt turkeys in the rain. And why I have a waterproof blind that I inhabit on rainy days if I get the inclination to go. Which is not often.

I would learn in the years to come that a rainstorm would often cause a gobbler to hunker down and wait out the storm. It assumes the "rain posture" says the biologists and just stands there. It certainly tends to dampen the mating urge and shut down the gobbling. But you can use the rain to your advantage.

I believe it was Jim Spencer, but it could have been John Trout, I can't remember for sure, who told me what to do when a rainstorm arrives suddenly and screws up your conversation with a hot gobbler?

You stand up, raise your gun and walk straight towards the bird – if it is safe to do so, no other hunters around. More often than not, you will find it hunkered down and miserable. The noise of the rain will conceal your approach and the bird will not be expecting you – at least for a second or two, which is long enough to get off a shot. Jim or John, whomever, swears he has accomplished this feat.

I have yet to test this tactic out, since I now have the good sense to sit in a waterproof blind and stay dry, but it sounds as if it is worth a try. One thing I can tell you, from lots of rainstorms screwing up hot turkeys, if you just sit there and wait, you will be SOL and soaking wet most of the time. There are always exceptions to this rule.

In my decades of chasing wild turkeys, I have yet to kill a bird under these conditions. And, I ought to add that I have sat through several more tornadoes over the years. This I can tell you. Tornadoes will screw up a turkey hunt in a heartbeat. One minute you got turkeys roosted in the trees. The next minute they are gone. Where? Who the heck knows?

Well, I sat there for a little while and pondered my predicament. And like I said, I do not enjoy being soaking wet. So I got up and headed back to the truck to dry off and contemplate some more. Thankfully, I had remembered to bring a towel and toilet paper – the amenities. I stripped down and squeezed the water out of my clothes. I toweled off, put some dry clothes on, then drank some more coffee and munched on some Little Debbie cakes.

All in all, I had had a pretty good morning. I was alive. I had found a gobbling turkey right out of the chute. I had called to it and it gobbled back at me – a whole bunch. We had even reached the point of showdown, when you stop calling and wait for the bird to show up. But now it was over. It was time to quit.

Back in those days you had to quit hunting at noon. And I had to go home and work the next day. So I left Raccoon State Forest and headed back to Dayton. I would return the following weekend and try again before the season ended. This time I would check the weather forecast, bring a poncho and a plastic baggie for my box call, just in case.

As I mentioned before, it was not easy to shoot a turkey when you could only hunt a morning or two before the season ended. And if you were a rookie, green to the gills, a walking screw up machine of the first order, it was next to impossible. Alas, it took me three years to dispatch my first turkey. Which was a jake and slightly dumber than me. Three years of mistakes, misadventures and royal screw-ups. I had no help. No mentors or coaches. I had to learn everything on my own. But, it was fun learning.

Twenty some years later, I am still learning and turkey hunting is even more fun now than it was then. I still screw up every now and then. But not much and I have shot a lot of turkeys. I quit counting after number 50. I have missed my share of shots too.

As for signs, omens and such, I still see them. So far, they keep telling me to hunt wild turkeys and leave the ducks or lack thereof to Uncle Doug and his buddy, Wayne. Did I tell you about the time they drove clear across the country to Stuttgart, Arkansas, the duck hunting Mecca, and shot only one duck? A piddling piss-ant wood duck. We have tons of them in the swamps around here and shoot them all the time. Ain't the irony sweet?

While they were in Arkansas, I did receive an important omen. Five wood ducks flew over my house three times. Or was it three wood ducks five times? Anyhow, I interpreted this sign at the time as a message to hunt in three states and dispatch five fall gobblers, which would be a personal record. And I proceeded to do just that. True story. Next book. ↓↓

The Swamp Daddy, a 21-pound Pender County bird. Taxidermy and photo by the author.

It took me nine hours to kill this bird. The story follows in the next chapter.

CHAPTER TWO

"Swamp Daddy"
North Caroling Spring 2005

Swamp Daddy is gobbling on top of my roll-top desk, in the turkey den, right this very moment while I tap computer keys, words appear on the screen and I write its story. The 21-pound gobbler is stuffed, of course. Head and neck outstretched in the gobbling position. Fat body all puffed up. Tail feathers spread and wingtips worn from strutting. A heavy 12-inch beard dangles from its breast. Two-inch spurs, curved and sharp, glisten in the lamplight. Leaves, twigs and dead wood, taken from the kill site, decorate the stand. I tell you what, that turkey was one heck of a bird. One I will never forget and admire for a long time to come.

Daddy's presence in my room, instead of in the cypress swamp, is a tremendous tribute, a humble homage and a victorious veneration of our duel that transpired during the second week of the North Carolina spring season. A duel that I won obviously. A duel that almost did not happen.

I was exceedingly fortuitous to feel well enough that day to get up at 4 o'clock in the morning, drive 45 minutes to Pender County and meet up with Mr. Tucker at the parking lot near the fire tower. I had returned from Texas with sinus and ear infections, my reward for hunting Rios with my oldest son who had returned, safe and sound, from Iraq. Three shots in the butt, oral antibiotics and other expensive pills, kicked in and I felt much, much better. By no means 100 percent. But good enough to go hunting.

Those who know me, know that I do not pass up turkey season, spring or fall, unless I am really incapacitated or my wife says I can't go. Which has happened only once in our 34 years of wedded bliss and that was because our only daughter was getting married. It was a tough decision, nonetheless. Someone once advised me, "It is better to ask for forgiveness than to ask for permission." He was working on his third marriage. I was still on my first and I knew it was not. If I went turkey hunting against my wife's will, there would be no forgiveness. Just divorce papers. She would get the mine. I would get the shaft.

On the other hand, if I stayed home, pretended to be helpful and marry our daughter off, the little lady would be happy and, best of all, beholding. Big time. Sometimes you just have to make the supreme sacrifice, bite the bullet and take one for the team.

I put the Eliminator in the gun safe, packed away my camo clothes and gear and stayed home. I was not happy about the situation, but there would be better days to come. And, thank goodness, we had only one daughter. If she gets divorced and decides to re-marry, I will not attend the wedding if it is during turkey season, spring or fall. That is what I mean by beholding.

Fortuitously, the doctor saved the season. His medicine worked and about a week later I rendezvoused with Ryan Tucker, my Baptist preacher buddy at o-dark-thirty in the morning. He had hunted the area a week before and – I would figure this out later – he had tangled with the Swamp Daddy on that previous engagement.

Naturally, Preacher Tucker failed to elucidate, expostulate and otherwise extrapolate that critical information in its entirety. He simply stated that he had "worked a bird" in the location where he was now sending me that morning. It was too dark to see the twinkle in Tucker's eyes and smile on his face. But they were probably there.

I, on the other hand, was simply happy to be feeling better and able to hunt. I was content to oblige my partner and head in the suggested direction. If you can not trust a Baptist preacher, who can you trust? Forsooth, we split up. Tucker headed west and I headed north.

"Follow the dirt road until it ends," he advised. "You will find a chufa plot, turkey cocaine, all torn up. There should be a bird roosting close by." Naturally there was. Swamp Daddy.

A lifetime of following directions to places unknown and in the dark urged me on to my destination and my date with destiny. In the predawn darkness, I walked quietly along the sandy road, twisting through the river swamps, my red mini-light revealing the way. The old bent-neck Army surplus flashlight from the toolbox had long disappeared. One of the kids "borrowed" it and did not put it back where it belonged. So I bought one of those camouflaged new-fangled mini-lights to replace it. Which was a stupid thing to do.

The mini part was a good idea. The camouflage was not. It did not take long for my youngest son to "borrow" it and drop it in the woods. I made him look for it for an hour, which was another bad idea. What was I thinking? Here was a teen-ager who could not find his dirty clothes, stacked waist-high and in full sight on the floor of his bedroom. And I thought he could find a little flashlight? I eventually pitched in, but no luck.

"Dad, it was camouflaged and I can't find it."

Hello!   Camouflage flashlights, wallets, knives and other important accoutrements that you or one of your progeny can drop in the woods and never find are not good ideas. From that day forward, I switched to red, fluorescent orange and road-stripe yellow gear.   And I learned to hide the stuff from the kids or buy them their own gear.

About 20 minutes later, I arrived at the food plot, just as Tucker had described. I sized up the ground quickly, it was good and I found a suitable spot to sit and wait. Just one problem. This was public hunting ground and the hunting is always dicey. The chances of Goober showing up and screwing things up were solar - the sun rises each morning. An astronomical certainty.

One trick to hunting state land is to get there early. And we did. Ours were the first vehicles in the small parking lot. But, that does not always work. Some hunters are considerate and, seeing parked vehicles, they will seek out another spot. And there were plenty of other places to go that particular morning. Some folks, the smart ones, will do that. Howsumever, the dumb ones keep on coming. They just don't get it.

They ignore your vehicles. They squeeze their trucks in, slam the doors, make lots of noise and charge right into the woods. A bird gobbling in the distance always triggers a frenzy of heavy-duty stupid-itis. And the next thing you know, they bust right in, oblivious to the clear and present danger that there are hunters already in the woods and in all probability working the very bird that they hear and could shoot them by mistake. Hello! It happens every darn time. It is inevitable. A universal law. A heavy-duty case of Goober-itis.

Naturally, I am an exception to the rule. I was schooled by a master hunter, who through no fault of his own, got shot awhile back during the New York fall turkey season. The man is now the poster boy for Mr. Be Careful.

Forsooth, against my better judgment, but armed with cautious optimism and the promise of dispatching a decent bird, I continued to sit on the food plot and wait for something to go wrong. We were hunting on a Monday instead of the weekend – maybe fewer hunters were likely to show up. It was the middle of the season, too, and the lazy hunters had quit. Maybe, just maybe, the turkey gods would favor me that morning. After my Texas trip, I was overdue for a favor.

I sat, waited and assessed my fate up to that moment. I had ventured forth into the river swamp to an unknown spot but with the solid assurance from a reliable source of a gobbling tom nearby. The food plot was where Tucker had said it would be. But was the tom, too? An owl hoot would answer that question. But before I could oblige, the real deal hooted from the swamp, 100 yards off. A raucous gobble responded back. A deep, heavy gobble that shook the cypress trees. Yep, there was a tom nearby. About 75 yards nearby. Perfect.

At first light the gobbler announced its presence from its roost tree overlooking the food plot. A lone hen decoy waited in the chufa patch below. Around sunrise the gobbler would fly down and join it. That was the basic idea. I had staked the decoy strategically where the tom could see it and Goober could shoot it but not me. Just in case Goober happened to crash the party and get trigger happy. Which most Goobers are wont to do.

The gobbles were lusty and full, a longbeard for certain. They filled the silent swamp with jarring sound and awakened all the neighbors. Redwing black birds, wood ducks, herons and more owls joined the dawn orchestra. There was so much noise that, if I had been inclined to tree call and I was not, my soft yelps would have been drowned out. I resolved to sit and wait until the opportunity to call presented itself.

Minutes seem like hours when you wait for a gobbling tom to fly down. Time drags out. It seems as if the sun will never rise. But it does, so I prefer to listen and play my notes when my part in the music score arrives. Solos don't usually work.

Finally, the moment arrived, a lull, a pause, a full measure rest, and I was able to share a few sweet notes on my slate. Silence followed and I knew that the gobbler had heard the call. I could picture the bird, up on the limb, cocking its head in my direction and zeroing in on the location of the yelps. No more calling was needed. My part was played. The tom knew a hen was nearby, waiting in the food plot. In due time, the gobbler would fly down and strut his stuff. So far, so good. I sat and waited for the wing beats or the change in location of gobbles.

The sun rose about six thirty and the gobbler cranked up right on schedule. It was fly down time and I perked up. It put on quite a show. Gobbles and double gobbles. It was working hard to gobble up hens. Since I did not hear wing beats and the sun was up, I figured the bird had glided quietly down to the ground. It was now strutting, gobbling and waiting for a hen to arrive. I switched to my mouth call and proceeded to lay it on, thick and heavy. We're talking cuts and yelps, purrs and clucks. This hen was hot to trot and ready for the gobbler to come on over and visit. But, alas, the tom did not appear.

Since I was sitting in a great spot, feeling rested and comfortable, I was not inclined to run and gun. I was well-concealed with good shooting lanes on a hot food plot. You can not beat that. It was simply a matter of time before that particular tom or another bird, which could not help hear all the commotion, would show up. I was content to wait, watch and even doze a little. Sooner or later a turkey would appear.

Four hours later, I was still sitting in the same spot but a bit confused. During those four hours, every 30 minutes or so, the turkey would gobble from the same spot, more or less. Which led me to believe it was on the ground, strutting, waiting and still interested in my calling. That possibility kept me sitting there. A couple of times I was tempted to get up, sneak closer and check things out. But, the bird would gobble and I would respond. We would chit chat. Then silence. And more waiting.

Well, it got on to about 10:30 when I heard a great commotion in the direction of the gobbler. Wings flapping against air and tree limbs. Then the sound of a big turkey landing on the ground. *Kaplop!* What the heck! Was I hearing right? Then it dawned on me. That dad-blasted turkey had roosted in the tree all morning and had finally flown down. What a low-down sneaky darn thing to do! It had lodged up in that tree, out in the swamp, and waited for a hen to arrive below and in sight. For four long hours.

Now, mind you, hours do not matter to a turkey. They do not wear watches or tell time or read turkey hunting books for that matter. Time is a people invention. This devious bird had this routine down pat. It would sit up in that tree, gobble periodically and the hen, if there was one around and interested, would show up. The tom would fly down and well, do its thing. The funky monkey. The turkey tango. The pony baloney.

On the other hand, if an impatient hunter showed up instead of a hen, the gobbler would fly away, safe and sound. The bird was a survivor and it had a routine that had worked for a long time. But now it was definitely on the ground and gobbling again. So I poured it on one more time – cutting, yelping, purring, clucking. And the gobbler poured it right back. So I raised my shotgun, pointed it in the bird's direction and proceeded to wait. I figured it was finally going to come over and check things out.

Not exactly.

The tom gobbled again but this time it was farther away. The wary bird was walking away from me and off into the woods. Not so fast I muttered. I jumped up and proceeded to head in the direction of the bird. This bird was not going to yank my chain all morning, then walk off and get away with it. No sir, I headed right for it. When I arrived at the edge of the trees, the tom gobbled again. It was deeper in the woods and headed away. I sat down quickly and hit it with more calls. The gobbler responded hot and heavy and stopped. I raised my gun again and waited. Nothing.

Then the tom gobbled again from deeper in the swamp. It had walked away again, leaving me to sit and wonder. So I stood up and followed, careful not to expose myself. I slipped behind the trees and pursued this onerous bird farther into the woods. Once again I closed the distance and fired the bird up. I sat down, gun up and waited. Again nothing.

Finally the tom gobbled again. It was deeper in the swamp and still walking away. Darn. Here we go again. We played this game of call, gobble and walk away for 45 minutes. I thought about trying to get ahead of the bird, a tactic which had worked in the past, but that was not possible. We were traveling on a narrow strip of dry land, not more than 50 yards wide in places, between two swamps full of water. I did not know how long the strip was or what was at the other end. This was my first time in this place.

It occurred to me that this particular turkey acted pretty "hawky," a term that Art, my New York turkey mentor, invented for skittish turkeys. It was an educated bird that had been called to a lot and probably shot at, too. It had a master's degree at least and more likely a Ph.D. And, the farther I pushed it up the strip of land, the farther away from the roost it would get and the higher the chances it might decide not to come back. Thus, a plan developed in my mind.

It was time to quit. I waited for the bird to gobble again. It had moved farther away up the strip of land. So I slipped quietly out of the swamp, backtracking and returned to the spot where the bird had flown down. I sized up the surroundings and realized that the dry land narrowed even more and created a natural bottleneck. Deer hunters call this a funnel. If that turkey returned to its roost in the afternoon, it would have to pass through the funnel. And I would be waiting.

Thus, I returned to the food plot, picked up the decoy and headed to my Jeep. It was about noon. I had messed with that bird for six hours. I was hungry and needed a break. But I now had a plan, a good one. I was not ready to surrender and go home. Just take a break. So I drove to town, bought some cheeseburgers, ate them and read the paper. I also called Tucker on his cell phone because he had left before me and gone back to work. I filled him in on what had happened and he said he thought my plan was a good one.

After lunch, I returned to the spot and sneaked into the funnel. I found a perfect tree to sit against, quickly cut some branches and stuck them in the ground. The swamp was about five yards behind me, which limited that avenue of return. And, I could see everything out in front of me. Most important of all, I would not call. Just silence. I did not want that turkey to know that I was there. If it was still around, it would come back and walk right in front of me. Sooner or later.

So, I mulled the plan over as I sat and waited. Yep, it ought to work. I was well hidden in a good spot and, as far as I could tell, I got there without being seen or heard. Hopefully, the turkey had not yet returned. Since the gobbler did not know from our morning encounter if I was a hen or a hunter, it should not be afraid to return to its roost. The more I pondered on it the more I thought I had that old gobbler fooled. It gobbled its head off all morning and the human hen it heard never showed up. Neither did a hunter. That old tom did not know for sure what was up and it looked as if I had a slight edge. I, on the other hand, had a pretty good idea of what was up and would use that to my advantage.

The thing about plans is the simpler the better. The more complicated the plan, the higher the chances of screwing up. Tom Kelly writes that "turkey hunting is an exercise in outdoor tactics where you have to make split-second decisions that are almost always irreversible." I would add keep the tactics simple. KISS. Hiding, sitting and waiting is about as simple as you can get.

Yep, the way I figured it there were two key ingredients. One, I had sneaked back undetected. And I would hide and remain silent. No calling. No owl hooting. No crow calling. I did not want that turkey to suspect anything. Second, the turkey needed to still be on that strip of dry land with a strong desire to return to its roost sometime that afternoon. The sooner, the better.

So I sat and waited. I dozed off a couple of times but I am a light sleeper and the slightest noise would have awakened me. I checked my watch and it was 4 o'clock. I had been sitting there for two hours and hunting this particular turkey for eight hours. I started to dread having to wait until sunset and fly-up. But I was in too deep to quit. I thought to myself, "Boy, I sure wish that old turkey would gobble or something. I wish I knew where the heck it was." At that very instant, I kid you not, a barred owl hooted behind me in the swamp. "Who cooks for you?" And 50 yards away, the turkey gobbled! Thank you Mr. Owl! I owe you a big one.

I could not see the gobbler but I raised my 1300 and waited. A couple of seconds later, the tom appeared 30 yards away in the funnel and at the end of my shotgun barrel. It stood still, looked right at me and scrutinized the landscape. I mean to tell you that bird was one wary SOB. And I did not move, not a breath, not a blink of an eye. But I did manage to size up the bird and it was a dandy! I could see its long spurs and heavy beard. This tom was a big one and a veteran of many seasons. It was definitely the Swamp Daddy, king of the roost.

I squeezed the trigger and the turkey tumbled. The duel was finally over and I was whupped out. It was 4:30 and time to go home. I got up and inspected the bird. Tossed it over my shoulder and hiked back to the Jeep. It took nine hours to dispatch the Swamp Daddy. Not bad for a turkey hunter, long of tooth and short of breath.

In my younger days I loved to run and gun. If I ran into an educated turkey I would give it a try then leave and find an easier one. Now a days, I do not mind sitting and waiting. Maybe it is a Zen thing – you can chase the butterfly or you can sit and wait until it lights upon your shoulder.

I phoned Tucker on the way home to tell him the good news. He chuckled and said, "I have been sitting here in my office, waiting for you to call. Something just told me if anybody could kill that turkey, it would be you. Good job!"

And I thanked him for putting me on it. Maybe next season I can repay the kindness. ↓↓

CHAPTER THREE

"The Anointing"
Bow Hunt at Site M

The Bible tells us that anointing is a form of a special blessing. If that is the case, I have been blessed in a special way. I have earned the dubious distinction, the dastardly displeasure, the distasteful dishonor of being the depository of turkey turds falling directly upon my personal anatomy - on more than one occasion – while hunting wild turkeys. I am not proud of this fact, but it is a known fact nonetheless.

As far as I know, I am the only turkey hunter in existence to whom this has happened – not once but twice! I guess that makes me a living legend, as they say, at least in my own mind. You would think that I would have learned to avoid the situation after the first turkey anointed me. Well, obviously I did not. It took two times. And if memory serves me and the truth wins out, I do believe there have also been many close calls.

On the other hand, if you think about it, it is a badge of honor, a compliment, in a left-handed sort of way. Does it not take great competence and surreptitiousness to steal into a roost full of turkeys undetected? And sit down amongst them and directly below them? I rest my case. However, I must admit that I do not deserve all the credit. My anointed status was not the result of a self-taught talent as are many of my abilities. This one I learned from a certain western New York turkey hunter, Art Kibbe, the Gobble Meister, from Sinclairville. Art taught me how to sneak up on roosting turkeys and enjoy the reward of watching them at close range when they wake up and do their limb aerobics. Wild turkeys are very entertaining all day long but especially first thing in the morning.

They wake up at first light and look around to see what's going on. They call softly to one another and stretch their necks and wings, I suppose getting the kinks out. And they relieve themselves prodigiously. Tail fans go up and "bombs away, look out below." The old saying comes to mind, "you can not do today's business until you take care of yesterday's." Turkeys are proficient at this. They have read the book. On one such morning, while hunting turkeys in Chautauqua County, Art and I observed a flock of birds hanging on for dear life in a dreadful windstorm. We had sneaked into Gobbler Corner in the dark, slipped up the hill to the upper blinds and sat down to wait and watch the birds close by.

A storm front had arrived, as predicted. The wind was cold and blowing hard – 40 miles an hour or better. The 50-foot trees in the corner swayed and twisted big time in the gale. The turkeys roosted overhead in the limbs hung on tight. It was a funny sight to see those birds, swinging, swaying and doing everything in their power to hold on. The wind was blowing so hard that the tree roots in the ground underneath my butt were lifting up and down. And so was I. The turkeys were swinging in wide arcs overhead like trapeze flyers in the circus. It was hilarious and I was amazed that they could even hold on.

Finally it got light enough for the turkeys to see that it was safe to fly down. And they could not get out of those trees fast enough. What was even more amusing than trapeze turkeys were tipsy turkeys. After they landed, they stumbled around dizzy. It reminded me of my grand son who loves to spin around, get dizzy and fall down. We watched this bunch of motion-drunk turkeys wobble around until they finally regained their balance and composure. Then they hotfooted it down the hill to the open grass field around the gas well, ignoring our calls the whole time. They had had enough of the woods, the trees, the wind and were in no mood to return.

Needless to say, we did not shoot a bird that morning. But we had a great time watching those birds and joking about them later as we drank coffee and ate Little Debbie snacks at the truck. In retrospect, that was probably one of the few times that turkeys did not defecate first thing in the morning. I figured they all suffered from a heavy-duty case of ass pucker while riding out the windstorm. I know I would have, if the situation had been reversed. I think it is referred to as "scared shitless."

Whenever we can, Art and I still love to sneak into a roost in the morning darkness and sit as close as we can. You can get too close and it can mess up your hunt. But, it is worth the risk just to watch wild turkeys up close. About half the time, they figure out what has happened and they fly down and go the other way. Every now and then, they don't seem to notice us and we get some great shots at gobbling and strutting toms early. You can not beat a gobbler flying down, practically landing in your lap and getting dispatched at close range. We call that a "wham-bam-thank-you-ma'am" hunt. They are pretty rare and a real gift when it happens.

I once killed a county-record tom, almost 26 pounds, in Missouri like that. The hunt was over before it hardly started. When that happens in New York, Art and I head back to the truck for coffee and sometimes to town for breakfast. It is sort of cool to arrive at the Superette's Hunter's Café and order breakfast early. The local folks figure we have shot a bird already and they ask us to share the story. Which is as much fun as shooting the turkey in the first place. Maybe more. Then they tell us where they have seen more turkeys and give us permission to hunt them.

At any rate, I do not believe that I am the only turkey hunter with the dubious distinction of being anointed by turkey doo-doo. Art probably has and Dave Chase, another ace New York hunter, too, for that matter. But they are smarter than me and will not admit to it. They are happy to point to me and laugh. I am the scapegoat. The only anointed one, so it seems, or am I?

Forsooth, after many years of pains-taking research I have discovered that there was another hunter, a Jim Bob Bubba Joe Crapper of Lickity Split, Arkansas, who shared in this affliction. Permit me to embellish this disquisition with his ancient fable of fecal fowl. Jim Bob Bubba Joe was a distant descendent of Sir Thomas Crapper, Prince Albert's plumber who invented the toilet. One day he went into the Ozarks looking for the rare and elusive Fu Turkey. You see, way back in those days, there were six subspecies of wild turkeys – eastern, osceola, rio grande, merriam, gould's and the greater fu – a chinese import.

The hillbillies who inhabited the Ozark hollers reminded him that if the bird happened to defecate upon his personal anatomy, he must not remove the bird dung. He must wear it. If he washed it off, he would die. Well, he was sitting under a tree, not paying attention, and a greater Fu was roosting in said tree. And it proceeded to crap upon his hisness. The smell was odiferous, foul, rank, ripe and otherwise malodorous. It is difficult to describe but imagine a combination of a chicken house full of ammoniated manure, a dairy barn full of slick cow muck and a waste pond at a hog farm. Multiply that by a thousand. That would be close.

Jim Bob Bubba Joe did not obey the mountain folk. He washed the mess off, promptly fell over and died. The moral of the story? If the Fu shits wear it? I don't think so. The moral of the story is – I was lucky. It could have been worse. I got bombed by eastern turkeys and their doo-doo is not deadly. It ain't pleasant but at least I am alive and can still hunt turkeys. Plus, let the record clearly demonstrate that I am not the only turkey hunter to receive turkey turds upon his personal anatomy.

The greater Fu turkey is extinct. The last one was extirpated, as James Earl Kennamer, Ph.D., of NWTF fame, is wont to say, in 1910. Since its fecal material was deadly, first the government, in its infinite wisdom, spent millions of taxpayers' dollars studying it. After several scientists died from exposure and Congress appointed an independent bi-partisan counsel to study the study, costing more millions of dollars, the lawmakers passed legislation banning the bird. Washington sent FEMA to the Ozarks, which hired hunters to kill every bird they could find. And they did.

Today, folks who live in those parts will sometimes sit around their campfires at night, while coon hunting, drink moonshine and recount the days of the greater Fu and all the idiots who died from its deadly doo-doo. In those parts, the phrase "taking a crap" has taken on a whole different meaning. And if one of the locals says "Fu you, buddy" it is not a compliment.

The moral of this story leads us to the perils and pitfalls of bow hunting for fall turkeys in Illinois. Particularly, the time that I visited the woods at Site M, a chunk of state land due west of Springfield, Illinois, to bow hunt wild turkeys.

On that specific October morning I was supposed to be accompanied by my buddy, Mark Faull, who is now an important DA-type in Phoenix, Arizona. Mark backed out at the last minute and missed his chance at anointment. Said he was out all night on a case and had to catch up on his sleep. It was Mark's fault that I was bow hunting in the first place. He was the one who insisted I learn and he proceeded to teach me. I borrowed a bow that first season and Two Bears set it up for me. I must admit I took to shooting the bow quite easily and could hit the bullseye at 20 and 30 yards consistently.

Getting a bow permit to hunt fall turkeys was simple, pain-free, compared to all the bureaucratic crapola you had to go through to get a permit to hunt turkeys with a shotgun. You could purchase a resident bow permit over the counter and it was inexpensive. The bow season was generous. It began October 1 and ran through January 15. Plus, you could purchase two permits – two turkey tags, either sex.

Forsooth, bow hunting for turkeys in the fall was a good deal all the way around. And, we had lots of turkeys to hunt and great places to go. Site M featured about 25 square miles of excellent hunting habitat – trophy deer, quail, pheasant, dove, rabbit and wild turkey. Lots of wild turkeys. At that time, the permit to bow hunt at Site M was free. Site M is now named for a former governor, who may or my not be in jail, and I bet they charge a hefty fee just to drive by and look at it.

At any rate, back in the early days, bow hunting was free. There was plenty of territory in which to spread out and hunt. If I told you exactly where my favorite spots were and you figured you could go there and hunt today, you would be SOL. Most of my favorite spots are now underwater at the bottom of the new lake. Progress. Howsumever, my most super favorite spot is on high ground, should still be there and still hold lots of turkeys. Perhaps one day I could be persuaded, bribed or otherwise convinced to tell where it is.

As luck would have it, I was able to slip away from work early, drive out to Site M and slip into the woods to roost turkeys on the evening before the hunt. As the sun retreated in the western sky, a whole passel of birds appeared in the woods and proceeded to roost in two large oak trees on a nearby hillside. I watched them fly up and limb hop. When it got dark enough I sneaked back out and headed for my truck. Before I left the spot, I counted four oak trees in a row to use as a guide when I returned the next morning in the dark. The birds were roosted in the last two oak trees on the hillside. I would slip into the woods the next morning in the dark, sneak up to oak tree number two and sit down with my bow and wait.

I called Mark when I got home to tell him I had some birds lined up for us but he could not go. I said OK another time but I was going anyway. And I did. It rained that night but quit the next morning. The rain produced wet leaves and a condition conducive to sneaking into the roost site without a sound. And I did.

I parked my truck and crept into position without the slightest hint of being there. I sat down by what I thought was oak tree number two and proceeded to relax and doze a little. While sitting there in the dark, semi-asleep, a large object fell from the tree and smacked me on the shoulder. It felt hard and round like an acorn and I paid it no attention. About ten minutes later another "acorn" hit me on the same shoulder and bounced off. Again I paid it no mind and went back to dozing.

As the morning progressed, daylight arrived and illuminated the trees. I could recognize the dark shapes of turkeys roosted on several of the limbs. About that time another projectile fell from the limbs above me. This "acorn" hit me in the leg and splattered. It was not a nut and it stunk. It was a turkey turd, a wet and stinky one. What the heck?

I realized in an instant what had happened. I slowly raised my head up to take a peek – which was risky to do in retrospect lest I receive a wet and sticky turd in the face - and, lo and behold, I beheld three hen turkeys roosted above me. They were taking turns dropping turd bombs on me and they seemed to be enjoying it.

I managed to move my leg slowly out of the drop zone. But, the turds kept coming. I proceeded to mentally review the predicament. Obviously I had made a gross mathematical error in calculating my position. I was sitting under the wrong oak tree. An honest mistake. Arriving in the dark and slowly tip toeing into the woods, I had lost my bearings and had miscounted the oak trees. I was perched under tree number three instead of number two as planned.

Alas, all was not lost. I could wait until legal time, raise my bow carefully and shoot one of the offending birds right out of the tree. Right up the butt and off the limb. How's that for pay back? Turd down. Arrow back up. A fair trade in my book.

On the other hand, I postulated, if I happened to miss with my arrow and it continued upward, sooner or later that arrow would return to the ground. Gravity. I remembered the dumb Hiawatha poem we had to memorize in Miss Wolfe's senior English class. "I shot an arrow into the air, it fell to earth I know not where?" It went something like that. Heck, it's been 40 years since I was in that class.

And, with my luck, if I shot a darn arrow straight up at the most offensive turkey and I missed, the arrow would fall straight down. It would fall to earth and I would know where. On me or in me, as the case may be.

Furthermore, if I survived the shot in the first place, I would have a hard time explaining how I shot myself with an arrow in the second place. I was sure as heck too slow to get out of the way if I saw it coming down. Adding more insult to injury, it would be my misfortune to end up on one of those reality TV shows, where they feature the idiot in the hospital emergency room who has an axe stuck in his head and no idea how it happened.

"I don't know. I was sleeping and the next thing this axe fell from the sky."

Yep, I was between a rock and a hard place – stupid is and stupid does. I shoot an arrow straight up and the next thing I know I am sitting next to Mr. Axe Head in the ER. At least, I was able to butt scoot myself over and out of the turd landing zone. But every now and then a turd would fall, land close enough and splatter. The wet leaves seem to enhance the odor situation.

By this time, the turkeys knew I was beneath them and they did not like it. Shooting an arrow up in the air was not an option – a double-dumb. You do not compound one dumb act - sitting underneath roosting turkeys - by following with a second one, shooting an arrow straight up in the air. I figured I had two smart choices left.

One, I could sit there, wait and hope the birds run out of crap, fly down soon and land close enough for a shot. Or I could jump up, start yelling and try to bust the flock up. Then I could wait, call them back and hopefully get a shot. I had used both tactics successfully in the past. But, the way the birds were situated in the trees, chances were they would fly away together in the same direction, regroup quickly and leave me out of the picture completely.

So far, I had been sitting there for about an hour or two. The worst was over, no more turkey turds hitting me. But, the smell was beginning to intensify, stupefy and otherwise odorize. The birds were nervous and fidgety, which indicated that fly down was coming soon. I decided to wait a few more minutes.

Before long, the turkeys departed. Every last one of them rocketed out of the trees at top speed, headed east and did not land until they reached a big bean field on top of the hill, a quarter mile away. My hunt was over and I was relieved. SOL but relieved. So much for sitting, waiting and getting a close shot. I sneaked up the hill and watched the birds loafing around on the other side of the bean field. If turkeys could laugh, they were probably laughing now and pointing back to me.

Three hens, in particular, were telling their friends how much fun they had crapping on the turkey hunter who was stupid enough to sit under their tree. I managed a couple of yelps and kee-kee runs while I hid in the brush. The turkeys turned their tails and walked away. Insult to injury I would say.

I returned to the truck, attempted to clean my clothes as best I could and headed back to Springfield. I had to drive all the way home stinking of turkey dung. Open windows and fresh air did not help much. I stopped at Mark's house on the way back to fill him in on what he had missed and, with luck, partake of Trudy's homemade ham biscuits and coffee. Bless her heart, she felt sorry for me and kindly fixed some coffee and biscuits. But, I smelled so bad they made me eat out on the porch.

There was another time while hunting turkeys in the fall, with my buddy Keith Glad, a chemist from Indianapolis, when I received turkey droppings from a roosting bird. But, that is another story for another time.

Suffice it to say, I am not proud of these fecal anointings. On the other hand, I do not know any other turkey hunters who are crafty enough, sneaky enough, sly enough to get that close to turkeys undetected and receive anointment. I have seen a boatload of TV turkey hunters and I doubt that they could do it.

One exception, Michael Waddell. I watched that boy crawl out into a field on his belly to shoot a turkey. That is my kind of turkey hunter. I bet a bag full of Quaker Boy Split Quads that boy is anointed.

All things considered, getting bombed a time or two by a turkey turd is a small price to pay when it comes to watching all the birds I have observed up close. And with those up-close tactics, I have dispatched my share of spring and fall gobblers to boot. I have bumped the heck out of lots of birds, too.

Removing the turkey stink from your favorite hunting clothes is entirely a different matter and worth mention. It takes two trips through the washer, separate loads, hot water and extra soap. Your wife need not know why you are washing them before the season is over. Better yet, try to wash them when she is not at home. Trust me.

Finally, I am contemplating organizing a society or club or association for the anointed. First, we need other brave turkey hunters besides me to step forward and share their anointing stories. Then, we could invent a clever acronym. When my son was in Iraq, he was a TWOT – tankers without tanks. We could have special pins and hats made. A secret handshake and password. Elect officers and have an annual convention with a gorgeous babe jumping out of a chocolate cake in the shape of a J-Turd.

Sound like fun? Probably not. I figured as much. ↓↓

CHAPTER FOUR

"What's Luck Got To Do With It?"
Doc Lucky and Rose Brook Farm

Bubba tells Forest Gump, "you got your boiled shrimp, your fried shrimp, your shrimp gumbo, your shrimp cocktail, your barbecue shrimp, your shrimp scampi, your shrimp…" Bubba babbles on and on about shrimp.

When it comes to luck, you got your dumb luck, your beginner's luck, your blind luck, your luck of the Irish, your good luck, your bad luck, your SOL and so on. Luck, like shrimp, can be served in a variety of ways. The word, luck, is a strange word. It is from the Middle English word, luk, which means to bend. Today it means the seemingly chance happening of events, which affects one's fortune, lot or fate.

Sooner or later, even the best turkey hunter will run out of luck and get bent out of shape. It is bound to happen. It never fails. For example, poor old Eddie Salter, the TV turkey hunter, has shot at and missed more turkeys on TV than any body I know. Talk about bad luck. I can not stand to watch him anymore so I change the channel. It is too painful. Someone needs to shoot Eddie and put him out of his misery. They shoot horses don't they? Come to think about it, shoot me!

When my wife and I were sightseeing and fly-fishing in England and Scotland back in 1988, she told me "if I see another cathedral, I am going to shoot you." I wish she had. When it comes to outdoors TV shows, I surrender. Enough is enough. We get three outdoors channels on the satellite dish and there must be 400 hunting and fishing shows. You've seen one. You have seen them all. If I never see another outdoors TV show, I will die a happy man.

Unfortunately, the outdoors TV business is thriving and has sucked up all the dollars that used to fund books and magazines. We have replaced the literary greats - Ernest Hemingway, Ted Trueblood, Robert Traver, Ed Zern, A.J. McClane, Zane Grey, Havilah Babcock, Nash Buckingham, Archibald Rutledge, Tom Kelly, Gene Hill, Robert Ruark, to name a few of my favorites – with God-awful TV characters and crap. I mean pure, unadulterated stinkola.

"Stay tuned next week as me and Jim Bob Bubba Joe stalk man-eating caribou in Yukola, Siberia." No thanks. Unless, perchance Jim Bob Bubba Joe gets eaten.

To paraphrase Pat McManus, it is not fine and it is an unpleasant misery. So I do not watch outdoors TV anymore. Simple solution. I would rather watch Oprah and give myself a root canal with a Black and Decker drill at the same time.

And while I am on the subject, permit me to add, with all the darn technology out there you would think someone would offer cable or satellite TV that gives you your choice of channels. Heck, we get 190 channels and 185 of them suck big time. But since the History and Military channels and Fox News are locked in to the 190 package I am stuck having to pay for the whole shebang. And please, somebody blow up the darn HGTV network! I mean get some TNT, find out where the darn headquarters are and blow it to kingdom come.

My wife is addicted to this channel and she gets too many crazy ideas on how I need to fix up the house. First, I explain to her that it is TV and trick photography. Then I tell her that there ain't one darn project that she has seen that is as easy or as simple in real life as it is in Hollywood. So far my supplications have not worked. And now she sticks project lists on the refrigerator.

Ditto for the turkey hunting shows. Trick photography. It ain't that easy in real life. Except the time I saw Jim Casada miss a turkey while hunting with Harold Knight. That really did happen.

Anyhow, back to luck, once I figured out how to get turkeys close enough to shoot, which took awhile and more luck than skill, I could not miss. I hit every shot – 20 yards, 30 yards, all the way out to 50 yards. It was amazing and I earned the reputation of being a deadeye shot. After awhile, I began to believe the hype. I was good, but very lucky too.

Then it happened. It was bound to happen. I ran out of luck. I started missing turkeys. Shooting over them, under them, behind them, you name it, I did it. A case of Eddie Salter-itis, industrial strength and near-fatal if you don't do something about it. Ball players call it a slump and they tell you just to ride it out. What the heck do they know? I called it SOL – shit out of luck. And it sucks. Big time. Every time I miss a turkey, little voices in my head, which sound a lot like the Hee Haw gang, sing.

"Doom, despair, agony on me. Deep, dark depression, excessive misery. If it weren't for bad luck, I'd have no luck at all. Doom, despair, agony on me." My theme song.

Missing a shot hurts. I put too much time and energy into hunting a turkey to miss the shot. And don't give me that crap about being out in the woods and enjoying the darn scenery. Art calls it "fresh air and exercise." Heck, I can get all the fresh air and exercise I need walking from my house to my workshop in the backyard. When I hunt turkeys and one gets close enough and it is a decent longbeard I expect, as General Patton would say, "to shoot the son-of-a-bitch." Let's get that straight. And if I miss the shot or something screws it up, I ain't happy at all. If I wanted to bird watch I would get some fancy-ass binoculars, a bird book and priss around the woods. I go turkey hunting to shoot turkeys.

The older I get, the more determined I have become. Not shooting a turkey is just an excuse for not trying hard enough or for screwing up or both. My oldest son has a hard time understanding this. He thinks since I am old I should be satisfied to go out and enjoy the scenery. He tells me if I get a turkey, that's great Dad and be happy. If I do not dispatch one, that is great, too, and be happy. I don't think so, numb nut.

The way I see it, if I do not get a turkey I have probably screwed up and it is my own darn fault. And that makes me want to go out again and try harder. My Dad called that "whole-assed." He was fond of telling my brother and me we can do things half-assed or whole-assed. Whole-assed is better. Always.

Speaking of half-assed, I have known a few "half-assed" turkey hunters in my day. I recall the time I went with a certain law enforcement officer and his assistant to hunt spring gobblers in Menard County, Illinois. I will not name names because I might be able to sell a book here. I did not miss a turkey that morning but the police officer did and it hurt. It hurt almost as bad as me missing. We were hunting the late Jim Short's farm near Oakford. It was full of turkeys and we had two gobblers hammering away up the creek at dawn.

In the movie, Kelly's Heroes, the tankers get a chance to nail a German Tiger tank in the butt, which is the only way a M4 Sherman can put it out of action. Odd Ball orders the gunner to fire. The gun tube roars (that is tank talk) and the back end of the Tiger is splattered in pink paint. Kelly is not impressed. The next shell is a live round and it nails the Tiger. Fortuitously, the tankers had a second shot. If they had been turkey hunting, they would have been SOL.

Fast forward to Menard County. The spring morning was clear and a prickly 23 degrees. But it did not chill our zest. The fervor of opening day of turkey season consumed each of us. A torch that seared the fat of winter from the bones. We arrived under the cover of darkness, in plenty of time, and moved quietly up the hill above the creek. Mark and I had roosted a couple of dandy gobblers the evening before, via binoculars, and we were headed in their direction. Miraculously, we avoided bumping the birds out of the trees as we settled in.

Soon first light arrived but the turkeys roosted nearby did not gobble. However, up the creek a couple of birds cranked up and gobbled non-stop until sunrise. We sat tight and listened to the commotion. As much as I wanted to get up and circle the birds, three hunters could not risk moving without being seen by the birds. We sat tight and in torture but we had no choice. It was too light to move without bumping birds.

Finally, the birds flew down and I called to them softly but no gobbles came back. I called again. Nothing. We watched and waited and listened. Nothing. A half-hour passed and nothing stirred. The outlook was bleak but then the MOJO arrived. A car horn blasted from the blacktop about a mile to the north and the longbeards shock gobbled. The horn blew again. The birds gobbled back. I whipped out my Lynch box call and yelped and cutted like a horny hen clinging to the last minute of her sex life. The birds gobbled back and moved closer. They were hooked and on the way so I shut up and waited.

Lusty gobble after lusty gobble boomed forth from the woods. The toms closed in and it was a matter of seconds before they appeared. We focused our attention on the location of the sound.

"I see one," Mark said, "about 75 yards out." I strained but could not see it. Darn, Mark had good eyes. Ain't no human can see that well. But Mark had hawk eyes and could see wild turkeys when they were only teeny tiny dots in a cornfield. Miles away. I watched for movement and I saw it too. A tail fan. Next, a white head the size of a softball. The first bird had arrived and was in full strut about 60 yards out. Just out of range.

It glided through the trees, looking for the hen. It gobbled again and the ground shook beneath us. It was a dandy, a shooter, a biggun. A state record tom if ever there was one. I sat next to Mark. The other guy sat about 30 yards away on our left. Mark raised his shotgun and tracked the strutting gobbler, which was now about 50 yards away. Almost in range.

I whispered to Mark to wait a minute more, to let the bird get a little closer. Mark had the big bird at the end of his gun barrel. It was simply a matter of seconds. Just a few more yards and the big tom would step into a perfect line of fire and an extra full choke of number fours. *Kablam!*

A shot exploded from our left and the big gobbler jumped straight up into the air, wings flapping. The other guy had shot and missed! Darn. The tom hit the ground running. It stopped about 70 yards out, turned and putted various and sundry turkey obscenities at the shooter. It joined the second gobbler, which had witnessed the sad affair safely out of range. The two birds lingered awhile then walked away. Bye, bye, state record.

Like I said before, I put too much energy and time into turkey hunting to miss a shot or have somebody I am guiding miss a shot. It turns out that upon further examination, the other guy had failed to change chokes in his shotgun. A load of number sixes through an improved cylinder choke at 50 yards did little harm. Except to piss off the turkey and me.

The next turkey season I evened the score for Mark. I called a big bird in for him at Site M. One of those "wham-bam-thank-you-ma'am" hunts. And he did not miss. He knew better. The tom is flying on his wall in Scottsdale, Arizona. As for the other guy, I called in a big jake for him at the Swiss Hog farm and he shot it. He had learned his lesson, too.

Again, I digress, back to my bad luck, which is what I was writing about in the first place. Wasn't it? Way back when, my Grandpa Harmon put me on his knee – which was a bit uncomfortable since I was a teenager at the time.

"Which one are you, Billy or Andy?" He could not remember our names, my brother and me.

"Let me tell you about turkey hunting. The number one secret is beginner's luck. You can try all kinds of tricks but you can't beat beginner's luck. You take a 10-year-old hunting for the first time, with .410 shotgun, and he will shoot the biggest turkey ever. Never fails."

I was getting desperate and figured I needed to do something fast. I remembered Grandpa's advice so I invited a beginner to go turkey hunting – a new buddy, Jeff Bierman, DMD, FBH, of Sherman, Illinois. Jeff was my dentist and a FBH - Famous Bear Hunter. Something told me he might just want to try hunting wild turkeys. He was not a 10-year-old and the last thing I wanted to do was take a squirmy kid, wet behind the ears, anyway. I was not that desperate. But, Jeff was a rookie, a greenhorn at turkey hunting.

I figured anyone who could stalk a bear in the wilds of British Columbia and shoot it had to have grit, large testicles and a truck load of luck. You got your bear hunters, again on outdoors TV, who sit in a blind over a garbage dump and shoot hungry bears. Then you got your real bear hunters, who actually get on the ground, bear-level, stalk their prey and shoot them toe-to-toe, eye-to-eye. That is my kind of hunter, period. And I had a gut feeling that maybe some of Jeff's luck would rub off on me. Forsooth, I invited him to accompany me to Rose Brook Farm in Missouri to hunt spring turkeys. And he did!

Rose Brook was 700 acres of prime turkey habitat, pure turkey heaven on earth, located 10 miles west of Clarkton, Missouri and the Mississippi River. I was privileged to hunt there due to my wife's luck. She taught preschool in Springfield and her boss had a brother who managed the Limousine cattle operation on Rose Brook.

One Sunday afternoon, we drove over to meet her brother and size up the situation. Upon arrival, I met James Morris, who would later become a permanent fixture, albeit a thorn in my side, a real pain-in-the-ass nemesis, in my Missouri turkey hunting. James was a rabid college basketball fan and so was I. We had two things in common – we pulled for Duke and pulled against Kentucky. I was in like Flint and James gave me carte blanche to hunt turkeys at Rose Brook. That Sunday, he filled me in on all the turkeys and their habits. I was impressed and could not wait for the spring season to arrive.

Just one problem. My bad luck. Even if I located birds and worked them, could I hit them when I shot or would I continue to miss? And my gut told me that James was a hard-ass, with a warped sense of humor, and would enjoy rubbing it in if I did miss. He did. But, there were so many turkeys at Rose Brook that hunting there would turn out to be well worth the abuse. I figured, sooner or later, with those odds, the slump would end and I would shoot enough turkeys to keep James off my back.

To end the slump, I needed to bring in a ringer – Jeff – and we had to avoid mentioning that Jeff had graduated from Kentucky twice, under grad and dental. We managed to keep this a secret for several years.

Alas, Jeff and I left Springfield and drove to Pike County, Missouri on a beautiful spring afternoon. It was about an hour-and-a-half drive. We drove through Pike County, Illinois, crossed the Mighty Mississippi at Louisiana, Missouri. We stopped at Joe's Jug, an unusual store, on Georgia Avenue to purchase Jeff a license and then traveled 15 more miles to Rose Brook Farm.

I need to clue you in on Joe's Jug. It is a "unique" store. Joe sells gas, beer, booze, adult books, handguns, shotguns, fishing tackle, hunting gear, lottery tickets. He's got every sin in the Bible covered. He even had *Swank*, Doc Lucky's favorite magazine.

We arrived at Rose Brook, crossed the creek and entered through the back gate. Only fancy folks could use the front gate that led to the big house where Miss Rose lived. Turkey hunters were relegated to the back gate. We had no sooner passed through the gate when we spotted a huge gobbler loafing in the pasture next to the road. I stopped the Jeep and we watched it for awhile. I had never seen a gobbler in that pasture before and so close to the gate. I was impressed and so was Jeff. It was an obvious omen. Jeff's luck was already working and I told him so. It gets better.

After we dumped our stuff in the bunkhouse, which we had to ourselves in the early days before James's girlfriend kicked him out and he landed in the bunkhouse fulltime: Girlfriend – 1 and James – 0. We drove up the road between Hammer Hill and Fifteen Gobbler Hill. No sooner did we arrive in the gap between the hills that we spotted two big gobblers standing in the pasture beside the road!

By this time, Jeff's eyes were big and bugging out. He was pumped up. And so was I. A double omen of the first magnitude. My luck had changed already and we had not even begun to hunt. We watched the two gobblers stroll into the woods and into Goober's Valley as the evening sun began to disappear behind Hammer Knob. I told Jeff we would hunt those birds in the morning and he said "Great!" We drove back down the hill, left the farm and headed to town for supper.

After supper we returned to the bunkhouse, watched a classic cowboy movie on the satellite TV, got our gear ready and turned in for the night. Since I was prone to snore, I took the bed in the bedroom. Since Jeff was the rookie, he got the pullout sofa in the living room. We slept well and woke up five minutes before the alarm went off. We brewed coffee and micro-waved some ham biscuits. We dressed, left the bunkhouse and headed up the road in the Jeep to the gap.

Stars filled the sky. A crescent moon bathed the back pasture and Goober's Valley with soft light. Daybreak promised excellent weather, moderate temps, sunshine, blue sky and gentle breezes. Add the missing ingredient, lots of Missouri longbeards gobbling their heads off, and it would be a perfect morning to be alive and hunting turkeys.

We climbed over the fence and slipped into the back pasture. Since I was not sure where the two gobblers we had watched the night before had roosted, I did not want to charge into the woods lest I bump the heck out of them. I was, after all, a "good amateur" at bumping turkeys.

Playing it safe, we sat down on the edge of the pasture and waited for gobbling time. It arrived soon and the surrounding hills and woods boomed with birds gobbling everywhere. We must have heard 15 or more birds, which is typical in Missouri. But we did not hear any gobbling in Goober's Valley. That was not a good sign.

Nevertheless, we sat tight and waited. Nothing. We waited some more. Nothing. Finally the sun was up and the surrounding gobbling died down. I decided to call some into the valley. No response. Nothing. I was beginning to have my doubts about Doc's luck. We had watched two big toms waltz into the valley at sunset. They had to be there. They did not vanish into thin air. If they were still there, they obviously did not feel like gobbling.

Eventually, we got up and sneaked into the woods. We took it slow and easy, scanning the forest up ahead for movement. Before long, we arrived undetected at a spot in the creek bottom where I had hunted before, where Mark had dispatched a dandy jake the previous season. We sat down and waited.

I called softly on my slate every 10 minutes or so. Nothing. Eventually, we both relaxed and began to doze a little. I would wake up and call, then nod off again. My eyes were closed but my ears stayed open. Then, I heard familiar footsteps in the dry leaves - turkeys. I opened my eyes and, behold, four dandy longbeards approached our setup in single file from up the creek. They had heard my calls and had come in quietly, unannounced.

I carefully turned my head in the direction of Doc and *"psssst"* at him. He looked to be asleep, too. When he heard me, his eyes opened and I ever so discreetly pointed at the approaching turkeys with my index finger. He moved his eyes and looked. Holy Cow! But his gun was lying on the ground. He was SOL. He could not move or the birds would see him. They were close. In gun range.

I, howsumever, had my shotgun rested on my knee and pointed directly at the first gobbler. "So far, so good," the little voice in my head whispered. I quickly tried to think of a way to shoot the first bird and give Doc a chance to shoot a bird, too. A double was possible. The first turkey was 30 yards and closing. It had no idea we were even there. Neither did the other three birds tagging along.

Doc, nevertheless, was still in a pickle. His gun on the ground and he could not move a muscle. We were running out of time. Any second now, one set of eight turkey eyes was bound to see us. I had to shoot. And, with luck, Doc could grab his shotgun and get off a shot at a surprised turkey.

I aimed my Winchester 1300 at the first bird and pulled the trigger. *Kablam!* I missed. The gobbler spun around and ran for cover. Doc grabbed his shotgun and swung on the birds as they scurried back up the creek. He could not get a clear shot. Trees and brush block the birds as they escaped.

I sat there bewildered. I laid my gun on the ground and moaned. I mean I was devastated. I was ready to cry. I buried my face in my hat and groaned. I had missed a 25-yard shot, a clear, straight almost point blank shot. It was impossible to miss but I missed. I replayed the shot over in my mind and still could not believe I had missed. Were there pellets in my shell? Did I shoot high or low? What the heck happened?

I have replayed that shot many times in my mind over the years. I still can not figure out what went wrong. My best guess is that I must have lifted my head just enough to shoot over the bird. I had patterned my shotgun before the season and it was right on target. I reckon with an extra full choke at 25 yards the pattern is about the size of a softball, maybe a tad bigger. If you lift your head ever so slightly, that softball is likely to zip right over a turkey's head. That is my educated guess as to how I missed. I will never know for sure.

Doc and I finished out the day by trolling. Since it was his first visit to Rose Brook, we walked and called all over the farm so he could see the lay of the land. Quitting time was one o'clock and we trolled until then but no gobblers responded. When we got back to the bunkhouse, James arrived and chewed my ass out for missing. I felt bad enough as it was. I did not

need his help. "Turkeys – 1 and Preacher – 0."
James kept score. We cleaned up and headed
home. I had to go back to work the next day.

From that day until now, my luck has
changed for the better. Whenever I hunted with
Doc Lucky after that, we killed turkeys. Lots of
turkeys. We found birds when no one else could.
We called birds when no one else could. We
dispatched birds in grand fashion and often two
at a time. Sometimes we would not find birds or
get a good shot. But, that was a rare situation.
Doc returned with me to Rose Brook the
very next fall and we doubled on birds. He was
with me the next spring when I dispatched a
county-record gobbler. And, after Mark moved

to Arizona, he became my faithful compadre for many, many years.

This past spring was the first time we did not get to hunt together since the early Rose Brook days. His oldest daughter graduated from Butler in Indianapolis. But he managed to dispatch a Cass County longbeard in fine fashion with his bow at our honey hole on the Upper 125 farm.

I stopped using my 1300 after awhile. I shot a dandy fall gobbler at Rose Brook and a couple of birds in other states with it but I lost confidence in it after that. After the fall season was over, I happened to mention to my wife that I would like to get a new shotgun for Christmas, an 11-87 SPS. Close to Christmas she informed me that the local sporting goods store was having an early bird sale, one-day only, from 6 to 8 a.m. Everything would be marked down 40 percent. Including shotguns. With her blessing, I attended the sale and bought the new shotgun, which I christened The Eliminator, at dealer cost. How's that for good luck?

I rarely miss a turkey these days. The Eliminator is deadly. It is scoped to keep me from lifting my head. It sports a ported Briley super full choke, .665. It shoots a three-inch load of number fours out to 55 yards with knockdown deadly force. You put the Eliminator, Doc Lucky and me together and there ain't a turkey alive that's got a chance.

Yep, all things considered, taking Doc Lucky to Rose Brook was the smartest thing I have ever done when it comes to turkey hunting. His wife might not agree. But, hey, who cares? She can stay home with mine and watch HGTV!

I've got lots more Doc Lucky stories to tell and I can't wait to share them. Stay tuned. ↓↓

CHAPTER FIVE

"Timber!"
Hermit Dave and the Fallen Tree

Before I lived in Illinois and hunted with Doc Lucky, DMD, FBH, LTA (luckiest turkey hunter alive), I resided in Ohio, the Buckeye State, and hunted with Hermit Dave, JD, SOL, UTA (unluckiest turkey hunter alive). And before I hunted with Hermit Dave, I hunted wild turkeys with me – by myself. Alone, I embarked on a course in life, a journey of profound significance, that I will look back upon with fond memories and practically no regrets. By myself at first.

One day I figured it would be more fun to hunt with another hunter. I arranged for my oldest son, Heath, who had dislocated his thumb while playing varsity baseball, to hunt with me. All I had to do was bribe the coach with the promise of a fall pheasant hunt and Heath got three days medical leave to join me in Vinton County to hunt wild turkeys. That was his first turkey hunt if memory serves me. Another story for another time.

Since then we have had a difficult time hunting turkeys together. We have had to beg, borrow and steal time from the demands of my schedule and his four years at the Citadel, four years in the Third Infantry Division, six months in Kuwait, four years in the First Cavalry Division and one year in Iraq. He is presently attending the Naval Postgraduate School in Monterey, California, getting a master's degree in defense analysis and counter terrorism. We are hoping to hunt spring turkeys at Camp Roberts, just north of Paso Robles, where my Dad was stationed during WWII. I need to save some money for the plane ticket and steal some time off. Wish us luck.

Anyhow, I believe it was my second spring turkey season that I persuaded my favorite fly-fishing and pheasant-hunting buddy, Dave Stroh, attorney at law, native of Wapokoneta and all-around funny guy, to go turkey hunting. He will disagree if you ask him but he went turkey hunting with me, willingly, blissfully and without any reservations. "Of sound mind" is the legal term. He will argue differently and mutter something about fraud, negligence, habeas corpus, caveat emptor and posse commitatis. Dave knows the law. He graduated Magna cum

Dental Epidermal – by the skin of his teeth - from the Oliver Wendell Holmes Mobile School of Nasal Proctology and Taxidermy.

I once wrote that I carefully selected Dave to turkey hunt with me because he was truly gifted – in blather, drivel and obfuscation. He had two long suits – discretion and a two-tone, double-knit leisure from Sears. I figured if we did not dispatch a turkey or two, at least Dave would keep us entertained with his pithy outlook on life and witty comments in general. In dog talk, I think they call that biddable? Best of all, Dave possessed a most endearing quality – he would never blame me if things went wrong - which they were wont to do on a persistent and predictable basis in those "apprentice" years. Looking back, we were a blatant case of the blind leading the deaf. Walking, talking screw-ups in the flesh. The Three Stooges minus Curly.

I must admit, however, I set him up rather well to accept my solicitation. I took him along on a pre-season scouting trip to Raccoon State Forest. We slept in my van and nearly froze to death. But, bright and early the next morning, we awoke about five minutes before the darn alarm went off, pulled on our heavy coats and trolled for turkeys. At first light, the birds obliged and gobbled their heads off for 45 minutes. We located 18 different gobblers that morning as we walked along the ridge roads and I called. Dave was hooked from that moment on. Hooked is an understatement.

Like I said, it was pretty easy. It was all in the set-up. The next thing I know, Dave had bought a new shotgun, a new Trebark camouflage wardrobe, new turkey vest and 453 turkey calls of various and sundry persuasions. And all sorts of gizmos and gadgets related to turkey hunting. He was calling me everyday and asking questions about turkey hunting. And what the heck did I know? It was my second season and I didn't know sh-t from Shinola - the shoe polish. All I knew was that Dave had the turkey fever bad, a terminal case. The cure was to take him hunting before he died of anticipation. So I did. Since I had created the problem, it was my duty to provide a solution.

The day before opening day, we drove my van from Dayton down to McArthur and the scene of the crime. We found a great site, just off the dirt road in the creek bottom, and set up camp. In those days, the legendary Steele's Motel, home of saggy beds and wet showers, was closed. If I wanted to kill a turkey, I had figured out from the previous season that I needed to string three or four mornings together. Dr. Turkey, Lovett Williams, had told me that.

He had written that it was next to impossible to kill a turkey on the first morning. I had tried and he was right. He said you needed to hunt a bird three or four mornings to be successful. To do that, you had to have a place to stay and the time to stay for three, maybe four days. Or, in this case, a place to camp. Thus, we camped. And that is where I made the near-fatal error, the faux pas magnifique. I mentioned to Dave that I was an Eagle Scout, Wood Badge Scoutmaster and an all-around master woodsman. I was born to camp. I could camp blindfolded, one arm tied behind my back, upside down and in a snowstorm. My middle name was camp. I was a master woodsman of the highest order. Silver Beaver, reporting for duty, Sir!

The trick to setting up a decent camp is to get there way before dark so you can see what the heck you are doing. We did that. We got there with plenty of time to set up the wall tent, cots, dining fly, chuck box, lanterns, folding chairs, wet bar, generator, TV, stereo, frig, all the right stuff to make our stay comfortable. When it came time to get a campfire going – did I tell you I was a master fire maker too? - I sent Dave off in the woods to pick up dead sticks and branches. We, master woodsmen, call that "squaw wood." And rookie turkey hunters pick up squaw wood. Master woodsmen and experienced turkey hunters chop down dead trees. We go for the big wood, the heavy-duty timber that will burn all night. That is what I did. I hiked up the hill above the campsite and searched for a suitable dead tree to chop down and saw into logs.

It did not take long to locate a perfect specimen. The tree was about 30-foot high, lots of branches and dead as a doornail. I commenced to chop away. *Whack! Whack!* Meanwhile, Dave continued to walk hunched over, pick up squaw wood and cradle it in his arms. Problem was he was walking directly below me and in the path of the dead tree when it fell. And it commenced to do just that. It proceeded to land directly on top of him. A split-second after the direct hit, I managed to meekly mutter, "Timber?" Too little, too late, numb nut. Talk about perfect timing. I did mention the Three Stooges minus one, didn't I?

The top of the dead tree landed on Dave, knocked him to the ground and dazed him a bit. Like the time 280-pound senior tackle Bo Taylor hit me with a blind-side block on a punt return while playing high school football. I did not know what had hit me. Just stars twinkling above my head, me lying on the field unable to breathe. In those days, we called that getting your bell rung. The team trainer arrived and asked me who the heck the president was? "Ding dong," I answered. What day was it? "Ding dong," I answered.

Dave recovered quickly from the impact, thank goodness, no concussion, no bells, and with a wit sharper than a rapier, he shouted, "Way to go master frigging woodsman! You almost killed me!" I was embarrassed to say the least. Truly repentant and heartily sorry I had felled the tree on him. I apologized profusely and tried to explain it was an accident. I had not seen him until it was too late and gravity was in charge. It was Isaac Newton's fault.

In hindsight, it could have been an act of God as they say in the insurance business. A test? Or simply a coincidence, that's all. I was looking at the tree and where the axe was striking lest I hit a body part. They teach you that in Woodsman 101 class. He was looking at the ground and for firewood. Neither one of us were looking at each other. I tell you what. That was the last time I chopped, sawed or otherwise cut a tree. I have turned in my axe and my master woodsman membership card and secret decoder. From that day on, I do not camp and hunt turkeys. I stay in a motel or at a friend's house. The axe stays home in the shed.

Well, I thought at first I had killed Dave, or at least did some permanent damage, which meant I would have to hunt turkeys alone the next day. Back to square one. But, fortuitously, I had not. He already behaved funny. He recovered and was able to hunt the next morning. He did complain of a headache and a sharp pain in the ass. Me.

That was the beginning of a wonderful relationship and sojourn in the Land of Oz hunting turkeys. I do believe Dave forgave me for my grievous transgression. I promised to wash the dirty dishes, clean the porta-potty, fold his toilet paper, make his bed and cook his meals for the duration of hunting camp. He locked my axe up in the car. After he pissed on it.

Which leads us to how Dave got his name, Pissing Axe. No, Hermit Dave. Remember Doug

Clark and the Hot Nuts? "Nuts, hot nuts, you get them from the peanut man." Ring a bell? They were a pretty risqué band back in my college days and they played the beach clubs, nightclubs and campuses on a regular basis. Compared to music and entertainment today, they were tame. Their records featured lots of raunchy songs and limericks. Barnacle Bill the Sailor? It's only me. I'm home from the sea. Said Barnacle Bill the Sailor. There was a song about a hermit named Dave, who lived in a cave and the money he saved? That was not how Dave got his name. Dave got his name because he is the only turkey hunter that I know who has shot a hermit gobbler.

According to Tom Kelly, of *Tenth Legion* fame, it takes some doing to kill a hermit. You see, a hermit gobbler is a feathered version of the recluse Howard Hughes. They do not gobble. They are not sociable. In most cases they are the very last gobblers left alive from a fall group of jakes. They prefer to be alone and left alone. Alas, they are virtually un-huntable. And no fun at a party.

I have had the misfortune to personally connect with five hermit gobblers so far in two decades of chasing turkeys. Dave's Hermit, the Heartbreaker, the Typewriter, the Hammer and U125. Except for Dave's bird, the other four died of old age. Long gone but not forgotten. Doc Lucky and I created U125 when we gunned down two of its brothers. Then my son-in-law and I bumped off number three. Which left old U125 all by its lonesome. And we dueled on and off for years. I spent the last four mornings of my last spring season in Illinois before moving back home to North Carolina trying to shoot U125. I lost the contest. His ghost wanders the woods and pastures of the Upper 125 farm in Cass County. A great story to share one of these days.

According to Dave, his hermit was a feeble old specimen, tall and skinny, with long curved spurs and a trophy beard. I had located the bird on our last Ohio hunt together a long time ago. And even messed with it a couple of times. But, I decided it was too tough a bird for me so I handed it off to Dave, who was just plain Dave at that time. Or Timber Dave in some circles. To everyone's incredulity and utter stupefaction Dave and the hermit connected. Call it fate. Destiny. Dumb luck. Whatever. And the rest is Ohio turkey history and fast becoming legend.

What makes this event so sensational is that Dave had the reputation of being the unluckiest turkey hunter on the planet. He bagged very few gobblers so we are talking about some paradoxical eschatology here. End of the world stuff. Cosmic significant stuff. I mean, the Red Sox win the World Series stuff. Forsooth, Hermit Dave got his name. He belongs to a very exclusive club with a limited membership. I will recount Dave's version of dispatching his Hermit forthwith. I have a copy of the text right in front of me but I will spice it up just a little.

The morning was wet, cold and windy – a typical spring day in southeastern Ohio. Having slept on the floor, Dave's back was in good shape and so was his mood. This was his kind of weather. He parked a half-mile from the roost and slowly made his way to a listening post. At first light a gobble answered a distant rumble of thunder. He knew the worst of the storm had passed and he sat against an oak with his back to the roost. Pinpointing the location of the gobbles would be difficult but verification of the bird's presence was all he needed. He figured it would head for the creek bottom and away from the wind. The time to strike would be when it came back to the ridge. That was the plan.

The next gobble sounded higher on the ridge, not lower. The bird was headed uphill and not down to the creek as he had expected. What was new about that? He decided to trail it at the base of the ridge as it went uphill. He also knew he would be in deep doo-doo if it got the advantage of elevation. He wanted to get higher but couldn't get ahead or around without being seen by the cagey old longbeard. He waited for the bird to make a mistake and turn back downhill.

The next gobble indicated that the old bird had found the wind at the top of the ridge too strong and it had turned back toward the creek bottom. Dave, on the other hand, figured he had to gain some altitude and he proceeded to climb uphill in a steep narrow ravine, slick from the rain.   Leaning on a burr oak to catch his breath and clean the mud from his boots, he gave a soft cluck to see if he could get a response.   An immediate gobble answered that question.   The bird was right above him at the top of the ravine.

He waited with rain hood down over his face and he listened to the bird gobbling, strutting, spitting and drumming.   It was close, less than 20 yards away.   He reflected on all the tricks I had taught him and immediately decided to ignore them.   Something told him that this bird was a hermit, the worst kind but the only game in town.   His heart pumped with heavy hopes and slim expectations until the next gobble revealed that the hermit was moving down toward the creek bottom.

Crawling and slipping his way to the top of the ravine, he wondered again where the bird was.   Then he heard a gobbler yelp down the ridge.   For a couple of seconds he reviewed all he had learned from me about hunting turkeys.   He ruled those tactics out.   This was a new game and he knew how to play it.   A soft gobble told him that the bird was near the bottom of the ridge.   Slinking from tree to bush to rock to tree, he closed the distance to 10 yards.   Every few minutes he would cluck softly on the slate inside his raincoat.   The gobbler would answer but not close the distance.   He spotted a small oak tree and decided to make his stand there.

He would be about 20 yards away, have a good field of fire and could see it coming.   The bird gobbled again and it was moving up the ravine to his left. Dave could not move without being seen. He thought what would the Preacher do, that is me, in this case? He knew the answer and chose a different strategy. He took a pushpin call from his vest and chucked it 15 yards down the ridge, hoping it would somehow land on the pin and make a cluck. One bounce, two bounces, three bounces a charm. The best cluck he had ever heard out of that call. A gobble answered back. And closer.

Next he pulled out his Lynch box call, held it firmly in his right hand and chucked it 20 yards down the ridge towards the gobbler. The rubber bands held the lid closed and it made a perfect cluck when it hit the ground. And, as it tumbled, it sounded just like a turkey scratching in the leaves. Two more gobbles echoed back. The next thing he knew, Dave could see the black shape of the old gobbler with the S-curved beard moving slowing toward him. There was too much brush for a clear right-hand shot, so Dave switched hands. Another gobbler was down in the ravine on his left and he could hear it walking in the leaves. He concentrated on the hermit and waited.

Two small bushes and a sapling were all that was between him and his moment of glory. Dave spied an opening in the brush and aimed his shotgun at the gobbler. The hermit raised it head from feeding and Dave's 1300 sent an invitation for the gobbler to go home with Dave –

a swarm of copper-plated sixes to the head and neck. Thus, Dave, in his own words, more or less, described his legendary accomplishment. The gobbler sported a 12-¼-inch beard. One and seventh eighths inch spurs. Dave writes that he does not need my help in dispatching turkeys anymore. He says all you have to do is just throw everything you got at them.

Thank you, Hermit Dave. How does that saying go? "No good deed goes unpunished." Hermit Dave was the first buddy I took turkey hunting. We spent a lot of time and energy learning how to hunt turkeys. We made a mountain of mistakes. We learned from some of them. We repeated most of them. We were a train-wreck waiting to happen back in those days.

Forsooth, 20 long and illustrious years have passed over the dam and under the bridge since our first trek into Oz. We both have learned much. We are older, wiser, long of tooth and short of breath. He has shaved his beard and I have grown mine. It is time for us to hunt together once again, Oh, Great Walking Eagle. How much trouble can two old farts get into while inhabiting a waterproof blind, kicking back in comfortable padded folding armchairs, sipping hot coffee, reading a book and waiting for a longbeard to show up? I rest my case.

I have extended an open-ended, non-refundable, lifetime invitation to Dave to come down to North Carolina and partake of our swamp gobblers. I promise on a stack of Quaker

Boy Pro-Triples that if he comes, we will not fall back on bad habits or hard times. We will not campout. He can sleep on the floor. He can throw all the calls he wants. And I will leave the axe in the shed. That sounds like a good deal to me. ↓↓

Art is very picky about where he parks his truck. In this photo, we are out in the middle of a pasture, way off the road and out of sight. We were hunting a fall flock of birds and did not want anyone to know where they were. This is called the hidden truck trick. Except you hide it out in the middle of a field. That way no one can guess which direction you have gone. Photo by author.

CHAPTER SIX

"Truck Time"
Little Debbie and Johnny Horton

Did I happen to mention that I was mistake-prone in my early years of turkey hunting? I seem to remember using the term screw-up a time or two. Does a walking screw-up machine ring a bell? I thought so. Flat head, slot in the middle, spiral grooves on my body. Yep, that was me. I hate screwing up while turkey hunting. When you mess up, most times the hunt is over, finished and concluded. I am not saying that your hunt with a particular turkey is completely over. However, it could be depending upon the magnitude of your screw-up. But, perhaps, you have just lost the first round, that's all. No matter, you best go back your corner - to the truck, wash down a Little Debbie cake with some lukewarm coffee, think of something different to try or head for another spot and new turkey. You have "screwed the pooch," a phrase my oldest son, the Major, taught me. Speaking of my oldest son, if you will permit me to stray a paragraph or two off subject, you might learn something.

It is a fine and pleasant state of mental health to have adult children, who have left the nest and are on their own. Psychologists tell us that today's young adults suffer from "delayed adolescence." This is an explanation and/or excuse for adult children to return home and bum off their parents.

Howsumever, in my family history, which reaches way back in English history to the Privetts listed in the Saxon Chronicles, and was continued in this country in 1664, all adult children leave home. I keep the family genealogy and it is a well-documented tradition. Page 1234 of the Chronicles states, "Hear ye and Forsooth, all Privetts must leave home thereupon reaching adulthood and return thereupon only if and whenst invited, preferably married and withith grand children, in that order."

I have shared this critical and ancient family document with the kids on numerous and sundry occasions and they have gotten the picture – wide screen, high definition, surround sound. Two of them are long gone and have their own homes and families. Number three has one semester left to finish college and graduate from the family financial plan. My wife and I are pleased with the way they have turned out and we have three grandchildren to spoil. And then we hand them back over to their parents.

When your kids leave home, the cash flow reverses and finally you can spend some hard-earned fluid assets on yourself and your spouse. There are plenty of leftovers in the refrigerator, plenty of beer and snack foods. You can find the darn TV remote and the wireless telephone. Heck, the darn telephone hardly ever rings and if it does it is for you. It is usually the kids checking in if they want to stay in our will. The peace and quiet is worth the wait.

And with adult children they can actually teach you a thing or two. Our oldest son hasn't taught me much yet about turkey hunting. I am still the senior officer in that battalion. But, he has taught me much about honor, valor, courage, leadership and service to his country and fellow soldiers. And, he has shared some unusual but useful expressions – "screwed the pooch," "beer goggles," "cluster f--k" and "good to go" to name a few. I appreciate his tutelage because it helps me stay in touch with his generation. I still prefer to keep my distance. But, I don't embarrass him too often around his friends. I can understand their language when I need to. Even toss in a phrase or two if needed.

Thus, in my early years of turkey hunting and using the lingua majorus, I was a proficient pooch screwer and consistent f--ker of clusters of the first order. Naturally, Hermit Dave, about whom you have read, was a great inspiration, too. I spent more time at the truck, eating Little Debbie cakes and drinking coffee, than in the woods with turkeys. Truck time gave me a chance to figure out what the heck went wrong, to decide what to do next and shoot some turkeys for a change.

In the grand scheme of things, truck time is important. I learned that from my mentor and inventor of TT, Art Kibbe of Sinclairville, New York. If one of those time motion experts – efficiency engineers, bean counters – ever ran the numbers on Art and me, she would discover that we have spent more truck time than woods time turkey hunting. But in turkey flesh, the truck time has produced many, many gobblers dispatched over the years. I would argue that truck time is a key element in turkey hunting and should be included in the efficiency formula.

I will always remember the first time I got the chance to hunt alone with Art and got my first lesson in truck time. Hermit Dave, my conjoined hunting buddy at the time, backed out at the last moment, as he was wont to do in those days, and stayed behind in Dayton. Dave offered some lame excuse to stay at home – his wife made him clean the oven, his new hunting dog had eaten the garage door or something pretty inadequate. I can not remember but it was the beginning of a long list of excuses that could fill a book. That would become a best seller today. I went anyway. I traveled to New York for my first fall turkey season and spent a life-changing week with Art. And I learned the value of truck time, which is known as "road hunting" in some circles. At first, I was confused about truck time but I finally figured it out.

On the first couple of trips to New York, I stayed with Al and Marge Brown over at Chautauqua Lake in their garage apartment. Their son, Brewster, was a good friend and faithful duck hunting buddy in those dreadful, gloomy pre-turkey years. A few years later, Art adopted me and I got to stay at his house in the village. Anyway, I slept well in the apartment and the next morning woke up about five minutes before the alarm. I put my hunting clothes on quickly, left the Lake apartment and drove over to Art's house.

On the way, I ran over a skunk at Kimball Stand. I slowed down to a crawl and tried to miss it but it double-backed under my rear wheel. I found out later at the Bean Pot café that a big coal truck flattened the skunk later. The nearby houses and gas station had to be evacuated because of the stink. Naturally, I played dumb and knew nothing about the skunk. We loaded up his truck and headed out to hunt fall turkeys. My first fall turkey hunt.

I have read somewhere that fall hunting was the only turkey hunting permitted in the old days. Spring hunting during mating season was not considered cricket. It was unfair to take advantage of spring gobblers while they were hot-to-trot and breeding. It was too easy. Since I am not near old enough to remember those days, I am not sure what hunters thought. But, it ain't ever been too easy. I know a lot of turkey hunters that enjoy fall turkey hunting just as much as spring hunting. I do too.

Most fall seasons allow for either-sex birds to be dispatched. But I prefer to take gobblers, preferably old ones, in the fall. I have only shot five fall hens to my knowledge in the past 20 years. Two of those on purpose – Thanksgiving dinners. One had a beard. The other hens were by accident.

Anyhow, the night before, Art had roosted a flock of birds in the gulf – which is Chautauqua County language for a great big ravine with a creek in the middle of it – behind Kenny Smith's house. We slipped up into the gulf in the dark and found a good spot to sit and wait. The turkeys flew down at sunrise or just before and Art tried to call the whole flock in but they went the other way.

I would later discover that Art could call a flock into gun range frequently. We did not have to use the typical fall tactic of busting up the flock very often. But on this morning, the birds walked away and headed deep into the gulf. The steep, rocky terrain prohibited us from catching up with the turkeys and busting the flock. Thus, it was truck time.

We hiked out of the gulf and returned to the truck. Out came the coffee and the Little

Debbie snacks and we postulated, pondered and otherwise cogitated on what had happened and what to do next. Art knew exactly what to do. We jumped in the truck and started driving. This was my first time riding with Art and I figured he had a definite destination in mind. So I sat there quietly, enjoyed the scenery as it passed by and listened to Johnny Horton fight the *Battle of New Orleans* on the tape player. As we drove over the back roads of the county, Art would point out the important sites in county turkey history and share the story.

"Over there," said Art, pointing to a large forest draped across the massive hill, "Uncle Mort and I killed our first gobblers." We turned right onto another county road and drove some more. Johnny Horton was now going north to Alaska.

"Up yonder," said Art, pointing to another patch of woods behind a postcard dairy farm, "I missed a big gobbler but Dan shot his first one. That patch over there is where Reuben and Henry hunt." We turned left onto another road and kept driving. Johnny Horton sang about the sinking the Bismarck. The tape was *The Best of Johnny Horton* all 15 songs. Over and over.

Well, the truck time went on for close to an hour – two times through the Horton tape. We covered a good chunk of the county north of the village. I learned enough about Art's family, turkey hunting friends and turkey history to fill a book on that ride. All the while, I could not help but think that the time in the truck took away from time in the woods, which is where the turkeys were and where we needed to be to shoot one, right? At this point, I should include an important piece of information. Art was a retired rural mail carrier, which meant he had mastered some peculiar driving habits. He had a propensity to ride the shoulder of the road and pull over suddenly to let faster vehicles pass us from behind. From the passenger side view, the road would disappear from time to time. Ditch banks and bottoms appeared close and detailed.

Although I knew to sit, watch and listen, I was confused at first and still figured we needed to be in the woods instead of the truck. Then it dawned on me, one of those ah-ah moments. I realized that I was receiving a great gift. The greatest gift one turkey hunter can pass on to another, the gift of personal hunting lore, gleaned from years of chasing turkeys, spring and fall.

From that first ride and 15 more years of riding in Art's truck, I have acquired an encyclopedia of Chautauqua County hunting lore. And I am inclined to sprinkle this lore, spice and seasoning, throughout my writing. To my knowledge there are only three turkey hunters who have received this great gift – Art's son Dan, Dave Chase a cousin and yours truly.

But the point here is that truck time is important time, a key ingredient in the recipe for success. I listened to Art and his stories and his turkey wisdom and hunting lore rubbed off. Over time my turkey successes began to outnumber my failures. The screw-ups tapered off and I shot more turkeys. I once read a description of turkey hunting in one of Tom Kelly's books. Tom wrote that when you turkey hunt you have "to make split-second decisions that are almost always irreversible." When I hunted without Art and would find myself in a Tom Kelly split-second irreversible situation, I would ask myself, "now what would Art do?" And that is exactly what I would do and it would work. Most of the time.

There is one more dividend to truck time. Art and I located many turkeys while riding the county roads. Art had permission to hunt 99 percent of the county. It is a bonus that comes with delivering mail and driving a school bus in the country. You know all the landowners and they appreciate getting their mail and kids on time. Forsooth, the truck time resulted directly in turkey time and we dispatched our share of birds, far and wide. Typically, we would spot a bird in a distant pasture or field, pull off the road and watch it. We would bail out of the truck, slip into the woods and hunt the bird.

One fine spring morning we happened to drive by Art's cousin Bill's farm and in the lower pasture was a big gobbler all by its lonesome. We pulled off the road, bailed out of the truck and sneaked into the woods. Art called the bird in and dispatched it in fine fashion. But, back to my first fall turkey in New York. Art and I spent quality time in his truck and visiting all his favorite turkey haunts. We located several flocks of birds and tried all sorts of tricks to call them in or bust them up. I will never forget one flock that saw us coming and took off running through the woods. Art and I started running after them but we did not have a chance of catching up.

Thus, it appeared that we would get plenty of "fresh air and exercise," as Art is wont to say, but no fall turkeys. Finally I suggested that we try a new spot – Al Brown's farm. Art knew Al Brown, too, through tree farming. In fact, it was Al who introduced me to Art in the first place. Although Art had permission to hunt Al's tree farm near Gerry, he had never hunted there. So we drove over to Gerry and the Brown farm.

When we arrived we found Al and his buddy, Ralph, cutting and burning brush. They had hunted turkeys for a little while earlier but it was time to work. Al said they had heard some birds early in the morning on the north side of the farm across the road and suggested we try there. We visited for awhile and then left Al and Ralph to their work. We drove over to the north side, parked the truck and headed into the woods. For an hour or so, we walked and trolled for turkeys. We would stop every 50 yards or so, call and listen. Nothing. We did spot a significant amount of turkey scratching in the leaves. Turkeys had been there earlier but where were they now?

We finally decided to quit and head back to the truck to get a snack, a drink and figure out what to do next. When we got to the truck, there was a note on the windshield under the wiper. It read, "gobbler on hill by cabin, Al." We headed for the cabin in the gulf on the south side of the farm.

Hermit Dave and I had stayed in that cabin the previous spring season. That was our first turkey hunt in New York and when we met Art. We would leave the cabin each morning in the dark, climb to the top of the hill and wait for Art. He would arrive and we would climb aboard and travel around the county looking for turkeys. We later discovered that there were turkeys roosting at the cabin. But, since we left before light and did not know how to roost turkeys in the evening, we had no idea they were there. The joke was on us.

Alas, it was time to even the score. We parked at the top of the hill and edge of the field and walked down into the woods. We reached the cabin and could see where a turkey had been scratching in the leaves. We sat down against a couple of trees about 40 yards apart. I sat looking east, Art west. We both called.

I had learned the kee-kee run by then and Art added great gobbler yelps. We would call and wait. I started to fall asleep. I was dog tired and plumb tuckered out from chasing fall turkeys for three days. It was all I could do to keep my eyes from closing and head from nodding. It was worse than English class after lunch with Mrs. Abbott in high school. And that was pretty bad until Bill Brendle showed me how to stack my books on the desk and hide behind them.

I finally talked myself into staying awake. It was getting late and the sun would set soon. All I had to do was buck up and pay attention. About that time I heard a loud cluck across the gulf and the adrenaline kicked in. Another cluck and loud purr. The sound of hoof beats in the leaves. Was it a turkey or a horse? Soon, I spotted a large turkey loping down the opposite hillside and headed right for me. Art kept calling behind me. I shut up, raised my shotgun and got ready. The gobbler ran down the hill and disappeared into the gulf below. I aimed the gun at where I thought it would re-appear on my side and there it was. Right in front of me. 20 yards. I pulled the trigger and the bird tumbled.

Art arrived quickly. He had not heard the bird or my shot. He was confused until he saw me stand up. Now he knew and a broad smile stretched across his face. We examined the gobbler and it was a dandy. I told him what had happened and he was pleased. I tossed the bird over my shoulder and we walked back to the truck.

My first fall season was over and it was a success. Not just fresh air, exercise and truck time. I had Thanksgiving dinner in the cooler. The bird weighed 18 pounds, with 10-inch beard and one-inch spurs. It was a fine specimen of a three-year-old tom. The tail fan and beard are displayed on my wall today.

I have shot many more fall gobblers since that October day in New York. I am proud of that day and grateful for the truck time Art bestowed on me. About three weeks later, my family ate that gobbler for Thanksgiving dinner. It was the first of many Thanksgivings that featured wild turkey, both liquid and solid. That hunt was a life-changing event for me. It solidified my passion for hunting wild turkeys.

Art Kibbe, truck time, Little Debbies, coffee, fall turkeys, first longbeard, spring turkeys, more longbeards. Like the TV commercial says, "priceless." ↓↓

CHAPTER SEVEN

"Adapt, Improvise & Overcome"
A Cass County Father-Son Double

My late father was the king of cliches. He had a word of wisdom or two for just about every situation. I remember seeing a book called "Momilies." My brother and I could write a similar book, titled "Dadisms." One of Dad's favorite sayings was "if you can't say anything good about somebody, don't say anything at all." I think he stole that from a Peter Rabbit book. I'm not sure. But, we heard that one a lot. The result was I learned to keep my mouth shut, ears open and give people the benefit of the doubt. Even when they were the biggest jerks you have ever met.

I recall one such walking rectum that pushed my good will to the limit. He was one of those smart-ass puzzle guys. You know, the brainteasers, the riddles, the Rubix cube types. Well, one day he saw me before I saw him and could escape. He had a puzzle he wanted me to solve. A piece of paper with dots on it in the shape of a square. I was supposed to connect the dots without lifting my pencil and end up with four straight lines. Well, I said I had a couple of minutes and would give it a try. I looked at the dots and just could not see how to solve it. Since I really did not give a crap about solving the puzzle, I quickly gave up.

"You got me, buddy," I said, "I guess I am just stupid." He responded with a snort-laugh and said you had to think outside the box. He took the pencil, drew four lines through all the dots. One of the lines went outside the box of dots. Obviously, he had attended one of those smart-ass management seminars.

I guess the point was that sometimes you have to think outside the box. Our encounter happened a long time ago. Since then I have heard "think outside of the box" a thousand times and I am getting sick of hearing it. At my stage in life, long of tooth, short of breath, married 34 years, three kids and three grand kids, I am darn lucky just to be able to think period. Box or no box. Life is too short to waste time fooling with riddles and puzzles. Hunting wild turkeys is challenge enough for me. And once I learned to think "outside the book" I started shooting turkeys. Turkey books that is.

Paul Simon sings in the song, *Kodachrome*, that it is a wonder he can think at all after all the crap he learned in high school. When I think about all the crap I read in how-to-hunt turkey books, it is a wonder I can think at all or shoot turkeys. In the early days, what the books said cost me several longbeards. For example, every book I read back then said you had to sit with your back up against a tree and you could not move a muscle. If the turkey came in from behind you, forget it. You were stuck and the hunt was over. I specifically remember reading that you could not turn around and shoot a turkey fast enough before it saw you and hightailed it out of there. I remember the author swearing on a stack of Quaker Boy Split Quads that he had tried this and the turkey won every time. Bull whacky!

I will never forget the big tom I called in while hunting in Raccoon State Forest. It ascended the steep part of the ravine instead of the easy slope, which I was facing. The book said that turkeys, like deer, would take the easy route. Wrong. Second, when the bird arrived at the top of the ridge and to my right, I was too scared to move. Although there was a large tree lying on the ground that would have blocked my movement, I froze. The tom walked by me and ended up behind me. It proceeded to strut, spit and drum. I sat there like a bump on a log, afraid to move a muscle. Finally, the bird walked away and I was SOL. The way I see it, the darn book cost me a nice gobbler that day.

A few years later, when confronted with a similar situation, I discovered if a bird ended up behind me and the cover was good, I could slowly turn my body, slip my gun out from the side of the tree and shoot the bird dead. I have used this tactic successfully many times. Thus, I have omitted the title of the book on purpose. I do not want anyone else to read it. It was written over 20 years ago and it should be out of print. And stay out of print. I still have it in my library but I will not go find it and tell you who wrote it. I would like to take the author turkey hunting sometime. I would take him to some remote place, leave him in the woods and he would have to walk back home. Pay back.

Needless to say, I have learned to adapt, improvise and overcome. In the movie, *Heartbreak Ridge*, Clint Eastwood tells his marines they must learn these skills. This is true in turkey hunting. Many of my trophy toms have resulted from me forgetting about the book and inventing new and unorthodox tactics. Fair and legal and safe, but just not in the standard manuals. I am not alone in this either. I watched the TV turkey hunter, Michael Waddell, once crawl on his belly out into an open field in order to close the distance and shoot a turkey. While he crawled he had the gumption to call too. The tom just stood there and watched him approach. When Michael got close enough, he shot the tom. There you go. I don't remember reading about that in a book.

It was because we could adapt, improvise and overcome that my oldest son and I shot two gobblers one Saturday in Cass County, Illinois.

Heath was stationed at Fort Knox, Kentucky at the time while he was a captain and in Advanced Armor school. He got a weekend off and was able to drive up to Springfield and hunt spring gobblers with me. As I have mentioned before, our times to hunt together were few and far between due to his service obligations and my work schedule. He arrived on a Friday evening and we could hunt together the next morning only. I had to work on Sunday. He had to return to Fort Knox on Sunday. Talk about pressure. It would take a miracle for either one of us to dispatch a longbeard with only one morning to hunt together. It would take a major apocalyptic event, for both of us to shoot birds.

On Saturday morning we headed out to the Kirchner Farm, my private hunt club, near Chandlerville. We arrived in plenty of time to hike back into the woods and set up on a gobbler I had roosted the evening before. After we got situated and first light arrived, several gobblers cranked up in the creek bottom. However, the bird I had roosted had lockjaw. No gobbles. Nothing. All around us gobblers hammered their heads off. It did not look good at all. By sunrise several birds had flown down and gobbled some more. The bird I had roosted was nowhere to be found or heard. It was gone. Missing. Evaporated.

I grabbed Heath and we headed up the hill and through the woods for the cornfield at the top. The morning was still early and I figured we had a good chance that a gobbler might show up there sooner or later. We got there without bumping any birds and sat together under a large oak tree. I stuck a lone hen decoy in the field about 20 yards away. We waited and listened while I called. Before long a gobbler answered back from behind us on the hillside we had just hiked up. The bird and I commenced to communicate - call and gobble, back and forth. It looked like we just might get lucky. The gobbler would gobble close and then get quiet. We would wait with guns up. Nothing.

Then it would gobble again farther away. I would call back. It would gobble and slowly move closer. But it would not come in. It hung up 50 yards away on the hillside behind us. After about 30 minutes, I had had enough. I told Heath it was time to speed things up. It was time to adapt and improvise.

When the bird gobbled farther away again, we got up and sneaked quietly down the path on the top of the ridge we had climbed earlier. When I figured we had gone far enough, I made a sharp right turn off the path and crept to the crest of the ridge. Heath was right behind me. I figured that the tom was doing what I call the "yo-yo" on us. It would get close, gobble, then walk away, staying on the backside of the ridge. Then, about 100 yards out it would gobble again. I would call and it would come back. Then walk away again. This time we "yo-yoed" too and would be waiting for it.

Anyway, I crawled up to a dead tree and slowly stood up behind it. Heath crouched behind a bush close to my rear. I cautiously shouldered my shotgun and poked it out from the side of the tree. I peered into the scope and saw the gobbler below. That was when instinct took over. I did not think. I just acted. I yelped at the gobbler. It gobbled back. A clear shot. I pulled the trigger. The bird tumbled down the hill. Dead. I turned to Heath who had witnessed the whole thing. It dawned on me that I had shot the bird instead of trying to call it in and let him shoot it. I just did not think. I reacted.

"Jeez, son," I said embarrassed. "I didn't mean to shoot that bird. I wanted you to shoot it. It was just reflexes. I mean I see the bird, yelp, gobble, bam."

"That was a great shot, Dad!" Heath exclaimed. "It must have been 50 yards. Darn, that was a great shot. Let's go get the bird."

We hiked down the hillside and retrieved the gobbler, which had rolled to the bottom. It was a 50-yard shot but the Eliminator, my 11-87 SPS, made those all the time. The turkey was a dandy three-year old, 20-pound plus, with one-inch spurs, 10-inch beard. I was pleased I had shot it but disappointed that Heath did not get it instead of me. I had plenty more days to hunt for my second Illinois tom. Heath did not. He had just a few hours left to hunt with me.

Naturally, he did not complain and was excited about my shot. But, I felt pretty bad and got to thinking. When we got back to the Jeep – truck time – we drank some coffee, ate some Little Debbie cakes and postulated, cogitated and contemplated our next move. Then, it hit me. The Upper 125 farm.

I told Heath I had a plan. I checked my watch and we had time. We still had a good chance to get him a decent bird. We would head for the Happy Valley at the Upper 125 farm on the bluffs just outside Beardstown. A private farm that only I had permission to hunt. We tossed our stuff in the Jeep and drove off in a hurry. Twenty minutes later we arrived at the farm and drove up the hill to the top pasture. We did not see any gobblers out in the fields or pastures on the way up but that was OK. We were headed for Happy Valley, a small 10-acre pasture nestled in a creek bottom that bordered the neighbor's farm on the east.

The Valley was not much to look at size wise but, for some reason, the turkeys loved it. We were careful not to over-hunt it and as a result we took three to four big toms a season from this spot.

Joe Hutto wrote in *Illuminations in the Flatwoods* that turkeys sometimes like particular places because they are simply pretty. I guess he knew what he was talking about. Hutto hatched some wild turkey eggs, raised the brood and lived with them while they grew up. He wrote about his experiences, which are very "illuminating" to say the least. I don't know about you but the whole thing sounds a bit kooky to me.

I can just picture me telling my wife that I am going to spend the summer and fall living with wild turkeys and then write a book. She heads for the closet and gets out my straight jacket. She says I need to put it on because we are going on a little trip. To the funny farm.

Happy Valley was one of those pretty places and the turkeys loved it. So did Doc Lucky and I.

It had been two weeks since Doc Lucky and I had double-upped on two longbeards there. No one should have hunted the spot again and we had left two toms from the original four that we called in on opening day. Heath and I slipped into position in the brush at the top of the pasture, looking down into the creek bottom and the rest of the field. On our left was a chunk of woods. At the bottom was the neighbor's field, grown up in weeds, then more woods and the creek.

There was a shallow dip that ran across the pasture, east to west – an intervisibility line in military parlance or IV. On the west side was a steep hill that ran up to the farm road we had traveled to get to the top. The spot was pretty and out of the wind. I am sure that is why the birds liked it. Lots of days the pastures on the hilltops were cold and windy. The sun bathed Happy Valley. It was warm and pleasant.

So warm and pleasant that I proceeded to lay down and fall asleep. I told Heath to wake me if he saw anything. Before long, he grabbed my leg and said there was a hen in the pasture below. I perked up and we watched from our hidden location. I called softly on my slate and a large gobbler emerged from the neighbor's weed field. It proceeded to enter the pasture and strut for the hen. It was hard to compete against the real deal but I called softly every now and then.

The hen was not interested in the tom as it circled and circled. The gobbler was not interested in me or our decoy at the top of the hill. Finally, the hen headed for the woods and disappeared behind the dip, the IV, in the pasture. The tom followed the hen and disappeared, too.

I reached over and grabbed Heath and told him to speed things up. He looked at me surprised. What the heck? Speed things up?

"Take off your vest, gloves and head net. Take the Eliminator. And head straight for the tom," I said. "It can't see you while it is behind that dip. Stay low and close the range. We are the only ones here. It should be safe." He understood and followed my directions to a tee. I watched him run down the hill crouched over in a stalk. About 100 yards down the hill, he straightened up and aimed the shotgun. *Kablam!* The hen exploded out of the pasture and flew towards the woods. The gobbler did not follow suit. Heath spun around and threw up his arms – touchdown! Then he proceeded to retrieve the gobbler and walk back up the hill to me. It was about 11:30 a.m. Thirty minutes before quitting time. We had dispatched another gobbler.

The gobbler was another Illinois dandy. It weighed 23 pounds, had an 11-inch beard and inch-and-a-half spurs. It was bigger than mine was and I was happy. Heath was pretty pleased too. We headed back to the Jeep to relax, drink some coffee and enjoy the results of our endeavor. Like I said, it was a cosmic event, not just a miracle, for both of us to dispatch birds that morning. Especially since the first bird had evaporated from the roost and things looked pretty bleak in the beginning.

But, when you are turkey hunting you never know what is going to happen. You can "go from the outhouse to the penthouse" in a matter of minutes. I coined this phrase many years ago in my *Tailfeathers* newsletter, which was sent to lots of outdoor writers and friends. Every now and then I hear it used on TV by some of the folks, who were on my mailing list. Is imitation the best form of flattery or what?

The Valley came through again and produced another fine trophy. It also helped to "speed things up." At the end of the season, I would head back to Happy Valley one more time with my son-in-law. And he would dispatch another trophy tom. Brock's gobbler came into my calls and we did not have to speed things up. We did have to improvise a little, however, and close the distance. But the gobbler came through the neighbor's weed field and we were waiting in the tree line.

What follows is called a disclaimer. I would not recommend speeding things up if you are hunting on public land or with other hunters. It is not safe to get up and charge after turkeys if there are other hunters in the woods. It is safer to sit tight, back against the tree and try to call the bird in. If you must move, you must be satisfied that it is safe to do so. Both of our turkeys were shot on private land that morning and there were absolutely no other hunters present. It was only after I was satisfied that there were no other hunters present did I consider this tactic.

What we did was use the terrain to our advantage. In both situations we were able to move on the turkeys without being seen. One bird was on the opposite side of the hill and I used the crest of the hill to hide my stalk and get into range. Heath's gobbler disappeared behind the intervisibility line or dip in the pasture. He used that terrain feature to conceal his stalk. I have also learned to use terrain features successfully to hunt flocks of turkeys in the fall. Again, I was the only hunter in the area and it was safe to move on the birds.

The books say to sit tight because it is safe. And it is most of the time. Another hunter can still shoot you if your decoy is not positioned safely. The turkeys will see you if you are sitting in plain sight and can not sit still or hide your movements. On the other hand, there are times when you must adapt, improvise and overcome.

If I have to sit in one place and wait, I have learned to pick a good hot spot, take a blind or cut limbs with a clipper and make a blind. This way I can move my shotgun, turn my body and so forth without being seen and still get a good shot. Thus I eliminate off-hand shooting and painful body contortions.

All things considered, I believe it was my Dad who once said, "There is more than one way to skin a cat." The same goes for turkeys. But, above all, be safe! ↓↓

CHAPTER EIGHT

"Turkey Grouse"
The Case of the Enigmatic Galiforme

The folks who reside in Chautauqua County, the western-most county of New York State, are pretty darn extraordinary. If you get a chance to visit these parts, you will discover a remarkable slice of Americana. The Gobble Meister, Art Kibbe, says they are descendants of Vermont folks - solid, hardworking, dependable stock that migrated west for better farm land. They found fertile land in the hills and valleys south of Lake Erie. Broad, immense hills and sweeping valleys, which the glaciers carved from the earth in their retreat north long, long ago.

The county is rural and covered with forests and farms. Lots of state forest. Lots of dairy farms. You will find the wild turkey abundantly present throughout the chunks of hardwood, evergreen and wide-open pastures. A plethora of poultry. And, as you would expect, some of the country's elite turkey hunters call Chautauqua home. Hunters honed and skilled at the call, shotgun and longbeard.

Although folks did not discuss it much, and particularly not with strangers, it was common knowledge amongst the more seasoned Chautauqua County hunters that the wild turkey in their woods were not quite the same anymore. On frigid wintry nights, with snow banked as high as the roof outside, local hunters assembled in the Full Strut Bar and Grill to discuss their plight. Inside the cozy pub, warmed by a cheery wood fire and lit by its flame, the discussion would often end up on the Canadian side of the border. And about a new strain of wild turkey that had crossed the boundary and located in their beloved woods.

No doubt, Reuben declared with the sagacity of his years, the over-abundance of this new strain of turkey had created carrying capacity problems in Ontario. Provincial wildlife personnel had been re-distributing the surplus south. Henry disagreed and argued that the new turkey had just flown across the river and wandered its way south. No government conspiracy, just the natural course of events. Or maybe Polk was up to his old tricks again, countered the Gobble Meister. Remember the mysterious white gobbler he said he saw? Or was it the Koteras clan up their tricks again?

Be that as it may, and for whatever reason, any Chautauqua hunter worth his weight in Quaker Boy mouth calls or who had Dick Kirby's autograph would concede that something foul was afoot. And word must not get out that the turkeys were not as pure, not as unsullied, as they once were. Lest, God forbid, the eminent status of the county hunters suffer irreparable damage and the arrows of outrageous misfortune.

The actual discovery of this predicament transpired ten years ago to be exact, during the autumn turkey season. Ironically, it was made by an outsider, who lived to tell about it, and an insider, the Gobble Meister, who did not want to admit it was true. Coon Dog Dave Chase was partly to blame too. He had told Art and me where the turkeys were in the first place and we hunted them, in the second place. And, well, after that things have not been quite the same.

As was the custom in those days I traveled to the village to hunt with Art. But this particular autumn hunt seemed to be cursed from the moment it almost did NOT begin. Three funerals and a snow storm delayed my departure from Illinois. I finally got to leave and fortuitously arrived ahead of the next snow storm.

However, by the time I arrived the season had been open for almost two weeks, which meant the easy hunting was pretty much over. Most of the big flocks were broken up - at least the most visible and best known flocks. After two weeks of heavy pressure the turkeys still alive were educated and shut mouthed. As a result, the fellows who were still featherless hunted hard, practically all day from sunup to sundown. This would be Art's and my curse too. Miraculously, Art had located five dandy longbeards in a cornfield north of the village. And with the first snow on the ground, we figured we could track the gobblers easily. That was the plan.

I left Springfield at noon. The weather was clear and 30 degrees cold. When I reached Cleveland eight hours later I hit snow - lake-effect stuff. It petered out around Erie. I arrived at Art's house just after midnight. The porch light was on and I let myself in. The trip took 10 hours 43 minutes. I had covered 662 miles. Dog tired I carried my stuff to the bedroom at the top of the stairs and collapsed into the bed. I went right to sleep. Even the darn volunteer fire department siren, located just across the street, did not arouse me from my slumber.

The stairwell light, which Art flicked on and off, woke me up. 04:30 a.m. arrived too darn early that morning. I pulled myself out of the toasty warm bed and descended the stairs. I ducked into the bathroom and then to the kitchen for greetings and coffee. Art had been up awhile, puttering around, fixing coffee and making his breakfast - toast and peanut butter. We shared coffee and pleasant banter. Then it was time to get dressed and depart for the cornfield and woods with the five gobblers. Which we did post haste.

Foolhardily I had brought on this trip a newfangled bow, a PSE compound, with which to hunt. Since I had been consistent with the bow in Illinois - three shots and three misses - I figured I would try to miss at least one turkey in New York, too. What the heck? My reasoning made sense, sort of. When we had tracked birds in the snow on past hunts, the turkeys spotted us and ran off before we could get close. I simply planned to shoot long distance - well beyond shotgun range.

Dumb. Dumb. And dumber. A disastrous decision from the get go. And, as sure as one domino topples the next in line, when I picked up the bow instead of the shotgun an unchangeable course of events commenced. And it terminated with two longbeards tracked and cornered in a "pucker brush" thicket. Whereupon, one of the gobblers panicked and exploded skyward right smack dab in front of me and my silly bow as I was standing there, fly unzipped and peeing my initials in the snow. Perfect timing.

It would have been an easy one-handed shotgun shot. A typical pheasant rise at 15 yards. A shot I had made hundreds of times back home in the prairie grass. But with a bow? Forget it. You need both hands to work the bow. I once watched some TV hunter, a hotshot bow hunter miss pheasant in Iowa and should have gleaned a serviceable lesson right then and there. But I did not. And for reproof I was doomed to watch a 20-pound-plus gobbler, 12-inch beard dangling in the wind, fly safely away. And naturally, the dominos of destiny continued to tumble. I did not get another shot - bow or shotgun - at a trophy longbeard that season. Stands to reason. MOJO is a precious commodity. If you use it up right off the bat - say a 15-yard shot at a trophy longbeard - you are in deep doo-doo for the duration.

And, before I forget, a word about "pucker brush" is in order. It is tag alder. Art says he does not know why it is called this. But, I would advance this etiology. If you imprudently aspire to penetrate a thicket - which we attempted on two separate and foolish occasions while tracking gobblers in the snow - you will find yourself thoroughly swaddled in its limbs and branches, tangled in its above-ground roots and rendered completely immobile by the tenacious shrub. And, finally, in unadulterated frustration your butt hole puckers up.

I was born at night, but it was not last night, so after the "pucker brush" incident I ditched the bow like a blind date gone sour and returned to the shotgun. For the next four days, solid, sunup to sundown, we hunted the fields and woods in the vicinity of the five gobblers. Nothing but exercise, fresh air and excuses. Not one turkey between us. And I was running out of time. I had a half-day left before I had to return home. Enter Coon Dog Dave. Who at the time was just plain Dave.

It was 02:00 a.m. when I, a light sleeper, heard a steady tapping downstairs at Art's front door. I perked up and listened. Art got up and answered the door. It was plain Dave. He was coon hunting in the woods behind the Gay Mart. His hound had treed this great big coon. But Dave had run out of .22 ammunition, trying to dislodge, de-tree and dispatch the varmint, and he desperately needed some more. He had left the hound dog in charge of the coon and headed to Art's for assistance.

But, best of all, Dave also had located a mess of turkeys roosting in the ravine behind Gay Mart. Art obliged Dave the ammo and thanked him for the hot turkey tip. Dave headed back to the woods and the hound and the treed coon. Art and I went back to sleep.

Folks generally will tell you that Dave is OK. His parents did not drop him on his head when he was a baby. Without a doubt, he is one of the top deer and turkey hunters in the county. But I should explain his proclivity for hunting coon. Dave says it happened like this.

One day he up and got the notion to branch out and become a coon hunter. As he explained one evening at the Full Strut Bar & Grill, you can do all three easily. Hunt deer and turkey in the daytime. Coons at night. You can do without sleep, food and stuff like that. And the price for coon pelts was pretty good to boot. So, bless his heart, Dave got the notion and there was no stopping him.

First, he traveled down to Pennsylvania and bought him an inexpensive coon dog, which meant a young one with practically no experience. Next, he took the dog out one night to see what would happen. And to his surprise, nothing happened. The dog had absolutely no clue. Well, Dave figured some fast training was in order. So he went out and trapped him a raccoon and brought it home and tossed it into one of his empty tame turkey pens. Then he tossed in that young green coon dog.

And, as they were natural born enemies, they commenced to mix it up pretty good. Fur flying. Snarling. Growling. That sort of thing. Dave calmly stood outside the pen and waited. He figured he would hunt with whichever critter survived the fray. Fortuitously the hound emerged victorious. And from that day on, it knew exactly what to do in the woods at night. And Coon Dog Dave commenced to coon hunt with all the time and energy he could muster when he was not pursuing turkeys and deer.

At any rate, 04:30 a.m. arrived too darn early once again. I descended the stairs. Bathroom then coffee. Where was this Gay Mart I wanted to know? And what the heck was a Gay Mart? I did not like the sound of it. Art said to relax. It was a tire and auto repair store. I replied that the owner needed to change the name to something less confusing. Otherwise customers were bound to show up, with no intention of purchasing new tires or having their vehicles repaired. Art said to get dressed. It was not our problem.

We drove over to the Gay Mart and headed uphill to the chunk of woods where Coon Dog Dave had located the roosted turkeys. Coon Dog had told us to enter the ravine and travel up the creek. The turkeys were roosted on both sides of the draw, not far from a tent. A tent? Someone had camped in the ravine recently. And he had left the tent. Dave said he had whacked the tent with a stick and yelled at it. But no one was home.

We parked at the edge of the woods and climbed down into the wooded ravine. It was dark. We slowly worked our way up the creek until, sure enough, we saw a tent up ahead. It was beginning to get light and we crept along quietly, searching the trees above for roosting turkeys. Soon we spotted one, then another and another. Dave was right on the money about this one. Lots of turkeys were roosted on both sides of the ravine above the tent.

I whispered to Art that we needed to decide our tactics - find a spot, sit down and call at fly down or figure out how to break them up and call them back later? No sooner had the words left my mouth than the whole ravine erupted in a torrent of shotgun blasts. We dropped to our knees and watched as turkeys boiled out of the trees and flew in all directions. Obviously we were not the only ones who knew about the turkeys there.

The shooting did not last long. And the shooters did not show themselves. The turkeys were now thoroughly scattered throughout the woods. Forget calling them in after fly down. We exercised option two. We decided it was safe to wait and call the turkeys back. We climbed up the side of the ravine and sat down at the top. There we had a good view up and down the ravine and into the woods above. We waited 30 minutes or so until it was apparent from the silence that the other hunters had left for work probably. The quiet ended with *kee-kees* and *yelps* from the turkeys dispersed around us.

We commenced to call back and, lo and behold, from the ravine below, yelps and kee-kees AND gobbles returned. We had hit the jackpot. Soon the turkeys headed up the hill and toward us. Art sat down at the very top, flat ground, and covered the woods to the west of the ravine. I sat on the slope, just below Art and watched the ravine to the east. We both called and the turkeys headed our way. The birds hiked up a small finger that reached into the ravine, arrived at the top and approached Art's position. I could see them too. A few yards uphill above me. And they marched ahead single file and oblivious to any danger. Art mentioned later that a dandy longbeard led the way.

The entourage arrived, extremely close, and the Gobble Meister took aim at the longbeard. A dead tree full of limbs and branches prevented an immediate clear shot. The Meister waited. At the same time, I, not knowing Art's predicament or I would have waited, found myself squared off, eyeball-to-eyeball, with a decent-looking Jake uphill at 15 yards. The young gobbler had a fix on me. Neck up. Body erect. It was ready to sound the alarm. So, I dispatched it posthaste. The bird flopped and rolled down the bank. The rest of the turkeys got the heck out of there fast. Running and flying off. Including, of course, the big darn gobbler that Art wanted to shoot.

I retrieved the ill-fated jake and to my mortification discovered it was a bit less-than-normal. Although it appeared to be an eastern wild turkey, it was pretty darn scrawny. And when I picked it up it did not weigh much more than a pheasant. Something was definitely queer behind the Gay Mart. Tires and auto repairs or not. But I decided to keep my opinion to myself for the time being.

We moved to a new spot and finished out the hour in the ravine by almost calling the same group of turkeys back up the hill. They yelped and gobbled and answered our calls. They came halfway up the hill a couple of times. But they would not make the complete trip. Finally it was time to head back to Art's and take care of the dead turkey.

Back at Art's garage, I hung the jake on the scales. It weighed just shy of eight pounds. Art was shocked and examined the specimen closely. He did not like what he saw. And he did not say much either. Only mentioning he had heard that several hunters had tagged small turkeys that fall. I field-dressed the jake and iced it down in my cooler - which my wife fondly called the Turkey Coffin. We exchanged goodbyes and I headed home to Illinois.

On the way home I stopped off at the Superette Market and submitted the carcass to the rigorous scientific scrutiny of Scott "Double" Dibble, assistant manager and chief turkey examiner. And to make a long and slightly boring story short, it was inferred and deduced through DNA testing and hickory dousing that the wild turkey in question was not of the eastern variety. It was a dreaded Canadian Turkey Grouse, full-grown and mature. A smaller look-alike cousin to the wild turkey. And it appeared that the Chautauqua woods were slam full of these heinous hybrids. At least the woods behind the Gay Mart.

Which sort of left me high and dry and with a funny taste in my mouth. When I shared what had happened with my buddies back home, they could not resist the opportunity to ride me hard about my new NY state record - the smallest turkey ever shot. And when I would argue back that it was not a real turkey, but a Canadian turkey grouse, they would dig in the spurs and laugh louder.

Finally in exasperation, I retained the prestigious and perspicacious legal services of Hermit Dave Esquire, attorney at law and sagacious solicitor in the wiles and ways of wild turkey. Dave decided to litigate, adjudicate, bifurcate and arbitrate this case forthwith and thus subpoenaed the New York Department of Conservation for an official affidavit. The NYDEC replied therewith, and I quote, "there is no such thing as a Canadian turkey grouse nor did the Department have sex with anyone by that name," end of quote. This left me worse off than I was in the first place.

Be that as it may, my wife, bless her heart, in her own inimitable way offered to intervene and settle the conundrum once and for all. And for the reasonable price of new bedroom furniture. She would cook the turkey in question and serve it along with another larger bird on Thanksgiving Day. I agreed. And she did just that. And the buddies innocently ate their fill of turkey-grouse. ↓↓

CHAPTER NINE

"Virgin Turkeys"
Boondoggle in Athens County

There was a turkey hunter who was driving down a country road one day, looking for a good place to hunt, and his car broke down. He pulled over to the shoulder, got out and opened the hood to see what the matter was.

As he was studying the mechanical situation he heard a voice say, "Hey, did I tell you about the time I went turkey hunting in Texas? That was a great trip and I bagged two Rio longbeards."

The fellow turned around and looked but all he could see was a horse standing in the pasture, head hanging over the fence. The fellow went back to looking at the engine and wondering what the heck was wrong.

Again, he heard a voice, "Hey, did I tell you the time I went turkey hunting in Alabama? That was another great trip and I killed the biggest gobbler on the farm."

Again, the fellow turned around. Again all he could see was the horse. But, this time the horse opened its mouth and said, "And there was the time I went hunting with Hermit Dave and Bill in Athens County to hunt virgin turkeys. Wow! That was a boondoggle of the first Order!"

The fellow could not believe what he was seeing and hearing, an honest to goodness real live talking horse! He immediately thought of all the money he could make showing off the horse. He saw a farmhouse up the road and he headed for it as fast as he could. When he arrived he proceeded up to the front door and gave it a loud knock. The farmer opened the door and asked if he could help the guy out.

"Is that your horse down in the pasture there?" the man asked.

"Yep," replied the farmer.

"I don't care what price you ask," the man said. "I want to buy that horse."

"Well, I don't know," said the farmer. "I'm not sure I can sell it."

"I want that horse," said the man. "You name your price and I will pay it."

"Well, all right, I will sell it to you," said the farmer. "But there is one thing you need to know about that horse. He lies. He has never been to all those places he talks about."

Hermit Dave and I went to Athens County to hunt virgin turkeys. The horse lied. He was not with us. But, he should have been because it was a boondoggle of the first Order. Webster defines a boondoggle as a trip or project that turns out for the worse. You start off with a great idea, great plan, but when it actually happens everything goes wrong.

With my connections as an outdoor writer for the Dayton Daily News, I was able to obtain permission to hunt a farm in Athens County, Ohio, that was suppose to be full of virgin turkeys – wild turkeys that had never been hunted before. This is a turkey hunter's dream hunt. Just imagine a farm full of naïve, uneducated turkeys. Birds that have never seen a hunter or heard a turkey call. It was too good to be true.

The farm belonged to relatives of a friend of mine, a co-worker, and she fixed it so we could hunt there. As far as she and her relatives knew, no one had ever hunted the turkeys there. When Hermit Dave and I had found out we could hunt there, we thought we had won the lottery jackpot! We were fit to be tied. We could not wait until the weekend and head for the farm. We were finally going to shoot a wild turkey!

On our way down to Athens from Dayton, we discussed how much fun it would be to actually hunt on private land. We would work birds that had not been molested, irritated, educated or otherwise disturbed by hunters as they were on public land – Raccoon State Forest, to be specific. We were thinking shooting fish in a barrel fun. Turkeys hearing your calls and running into your set-up full speed. Shooting them in self-defense. Turkey hunting just like in the books. Gobbler in the tree, it flies down and comes in. Wham, bam, thank you, ma'am. Surely virgin turkeys would cure our lack of success.

Both of us suffered at the time from an ignominious malady known as *deja-vu-itis* - the chronic inflammation of the *here-we-go-again*. This disorder presented itself as an extremely fervent curse of the second-guess. It provoked Hermit Dave and I to always decide to decide once too often in the course of hunting turkeys. It resulted in us doing the same wrong darn thing over and over again.

I insisted that the likely cause of this ailment was our perusal of excessive amounts of spurious and inflated literature on the subject of wild turkey hunting. It was severely exacerbated by the inclination to listen too often to self-anointed "experts." And hunting only public land birds further irritated it. The cure was a dose of virgin turkeys - administered once a day in the morning on private land. Alas, we would be cured soon and our hopes were high.

We arrived in Athens and headed south of town, following Linda's directions. We located her uncle's farm easily, parked in the driveway and introduced ourselves. The Mansfields were expecting us, delighted to meet us and gave us permission to hunt on their farm. While we stood in the front yard and got acquainted, a turkey gobbled from top of the hill across the road. Uncle Earl pointed to the spot and said it was on his property. He added that the turkey gobbled up there every evening. Talk about luck. We had been there five minutes and already had a turkey roosted. From Uncle Earl's front yard.

We headed up the hill to check out the terrain before it got dark. When we got up there we could see Uncle Earl's front porch light down below in the valley. We did some quick triangulations and determined that the gobbler was roosting nearby. It was time to head to the motel in town, get some grub and a good night's sleep. Tomorrow would be best day of turkey hunting we had ever experienced. We were like kids on the last day of school before summer vacation.

The next morning we woke up five minutes before the alarm went off. We got up and put on our hunting clothes. Grabbed some hot coffee and Little Debbie rolls and headed to the farm. Our first virgin gobbler was waiting for us. All we had to do was get there in plenty of time and sneak into the woods in the dark. Sit down and wait. Piece of cake. A ten-year-old kid could do this blind folded. We parked the Jeep at the designated spot, slipped on our gear and quietly sneaked into the woods.

We had not gone very far and I stopped and whispered to Dave, "What do you think? Have we gone far enough?"

"Jeez, I don't know," Dave murmured. "What do you think?" About that time.

Whuup! Whuup! Whuup!

The gobbler busted out of the tree right in front of us and flew off. Did I mention that I was an expert in bumping gobblers out of trees in the dark? I thought so. And in hindsight, if we had managed to sit down quietly without bumping the bird, we would still have been too close to work the bird properly. It would have been roosting right over our heads and we probably would have been anointed with turkey turds.

"What do we do now, Master Woodsman?" Hermit Dave asked in a slightly perturbed voice.

"Well, the book says that when this happens we are suppose to sit down, wait till things settle down and try to call the gobbler back," said I. "But, before we do that I have to take a dump. Bad." I could feel the colon muscles spasm, which meant I had about two minutes to unload or I would need clean underwear.

While Hermit Dave carefully selected a proper set-up tree and staked out the decoys, I slipped off into the woods, down wind, and selected a "leaner" tree.

I once read in one of Tom Kelly's books that he was the only turkey hunter afflicted with this ailment. But he was mistaken. I know of at least three other hunters who have to crap five minutes after they hit the woods. Me. My brother-in-law Big Doug. I probably taught him this too. And Tony Knight, the humble gunsmith who made a zillion dollars inventing and selling the Knight muzzleloader rifle. I used to hunt turkeys with Tony at his old farm near Kirksville, Missouri. One afternoon we were sitting in the living room, watching Oprah on the old black and white TV. It only got one channel. Maybe it was what psychologists call a subliminal message but while watching Oprah the topic of crapping in the woods came up.

Tony stated that no matter what precautions he took, he had to crap in the woods five minutes after he got there. If he could only bottle it – the essence of woods – he could make another zillion dollars selling it as a laxative. I told him I had the same problem.

About that time, another guest arrived. He was the head banana of ATAC camouflage and they were at the farm to make a promotional video for the new camouflage pattern. Talk about being a bastard at a family picnic, I was the only hunter at Tony's farm that did not have new ATAC camouflage. I wore the new dark green Realtree pattern. The rest of the group, including Hermit Dave who was accompanying me, had this ATAC stuff.

Well, Tony remarked to the ATAC guy that his camouflage needed some green in it. The guy responded that they had developed this pattern down at Fort Campbell, Kentucky and it was based on solid scientific data. He then began to pontificate, prevaricate and otherwise postulate that animal eyes have different rods and cones and they do not see green. When they see the ATAC pattern they get dizzy and hence the hunter disappears. Tony replied that if the ATAC guys were selling this pattern to deer and turkeys it would not matter if it did not have any green. But, if they wanted hunters to buy it, they had better put some darn green in it.

The ATAC team hunted for four days with Toby Bridges as their guide. They did not kill a turkey. They left without a promotional video and some crappy camo that did not work. Furthermore, they ignored Tony's advice about green and subsequently went out of business. Every now and then, I see a picture of a hunter wearing ATAC camouflage. Probably bought it super cheap. A closeout.

Back to the point, Tom Kelly is not alone. I have identified three other hunters who can not hunt without crapping in the woods first. Perhaps, it is a genetic thing going back to cave men and their need to mark their territory. Who knows? But, when the urge arrives, I can not wait. I head for a decent tree, preferably a live one – dead ones tend to break when you are hanging on - and limber enough to bend while I lean back. The trick is to make sure your suspenders are not in the line of fire. Did that once. I don't wear suspenders any more. And I always carry striking paper. I once used leaves long ago when I as a Tenderfoot Scout and ended up with poison oak on my posterior. Not fun.

At any rate, Hermit Dave got settled in and I returned feeling much lighter and ready to hunt. We sat and waited for the sun to rise. The gobbler had flown only 50 yards away and had landed in another tree. We could see it and we called softly to it. It did not bother to gobble back. While we waited for this gobbler to do something, we heard another bird down in the valley below, close to the farmhouse, gobbling its head off. We made a mental note of its location for future reference.

Finally, our gobbler flew down, but not in our direction. Instead it disappeared down the ridge into a valley below us. We sat there for awhile longer and then got up to leave. This gobbler might have been a virgin but no more. We had screwed it up. Big time. Dave suggested we go to town, eat breakfast and let the bird settle down. We did.

After breakfast, we returned to the scene of the crime. We figured the gobbler was still down in the valley below so we sneaked into the woods above it and sat down on a terrain feature called a terrace or bench. We started calling and it answered back. Before long it fired up and moved closer. We started to feel better and to muster a little hope. However, if we had not read the book, which stated that we could not move and had to sit still with our backs to a tree, we would have figured out that one of us could have slipped up to the edge of the terrace while the other continued to call. Maybe even assumed the prone position, like Michael Waddell, and got a shot at the gobbler, which was now close and on the next ledge just below us. But no, we just sat there like dummies and waited for the bird to show. It did not. It finally got bored and left.

We left too and spent the rest of the morning walking around the farm, trolling for another virgin gobbler, getting the lay of the land and locating the place where the gobbler we had heard earlier had been. We quit around noon, headed back to town for a hot shower, more grub and a nap. Later that afternoon, we returned to the farm to the spot down in the valley near the farmhouse where we had heard a gobbler hammer its head off earlier that morning.

At this spot I proceeded to roost a ruffed grouse, thinking it was a turkey. Dave and I split up. I sat down in the woods where I thought the gobbler had been that morning. Around sunset, I heard wing beats close by and behind me. I froze lest I bump the bird. Finally, it got dark enough for me to slip away. I told Dave that I had roosted the bird and it would be a good bird to hunt in the morning.

We headed back to the motel, ate supper, watched TV and went to bed. We woke up the next morning and headed back to the farm. We decided to split up. Dave went one way. I went to the spot where I had roosted the turkey, so I thought. I found a suitable tree, sat down and waited.

Before long, as it was getting light, I heard footsteps behind me. They got closer and closer. They were right behind me and then I could see what it was. A red fox walked right by my tree so close that I could have reached out and touched it. It did not know I was there. Although I heard lots of gobbling up on the hill from the bird we had messed with the previous morning, I heard nothing where I was.

Finally, I heard wing beats and was I surprised to see a ruffed grouse land at my feet. Surprised and stupid. Across the road, where Dave was supposed to be, I heard a gobbler hammer its head off. The turkeys had roosted in the trees behind an abandoned farmhouse. I got up and headed in that direction.

By the time I arrived the birds had flown down and were headed off in the opposite direction. I followed them, calling with my Quaker Boy Pro Triple. The gobbler responded to every yelp and cutt, but the boss hen would fire up and lead the gobbler away. I pursued these birds for about 45 minutes with the same results every time. I would fire the tom up, it would come my way, the boss hen would start calling and the tom would go back to it. I finally surrendered and went looking for Dave.

I don't remember what Hermit Dave did that morning. I think he went back up the hill after the bird we had messed with the previous

137

morning. But he did not kill it. We did make an important discovery, however.

Dave ran into another hunter up on the hilltop that had hunted on the farm every morning. I met an elderly gentleman in the valley who had worked the turkey that we had heard gobbling in the valley below. Both of these hunters had hunted our "virgin turkeys" every morning of the season so far. We did not know whether to be pissed off or relieved. Maybe a little bit of both. We returned home after thanking our hosts and mentioning that they had poachers. Sadly, we realized that there ain't no such thing as a virgin turkey. Hunting on private land and competing with other hunters can be just as difficult as hunting on public land. Heck, the turkeys don't know the difference. It's just land to them.

Over the years I have pursued the elusive virgin turkey. Every now and then I would find one that was green. A wham-bam-thank-you ma'am bird. The back valley at Rose Brook farm in Missouri held lots of virgin birds. For a long time I was the only hunter who hunted them. I shot a lot of them too. Sadly that changed when Goober started to hunt there and mess the turkeys and me up. My challenge became shooting turkeys before Goober could get close and screw things up. I got pretty good at that.

I also dispatched my share of green birds on the Upper 125 farm in Cass County, Illinois.

Unfortunately, that farm has been sold and another hunt club has the lease.

As for boondoggles, I am getting better at avoiding them. I have learned to invoke the Uncle Doug Boondoggle Rule.

Doug suggests that we go somewhere and hunt.

I answer, "Let me think about it."

And I think to myself, "Is this worth the time, effort, cost, sitting in the cold or rain, getting lost or not shooting anything? Or is it another boondoggle?"

As a rule, I usually respond "I don't think so. Thanks anyway."

I think I am getting wiser in my old age and have reached my limit of boondoggles.

The last trip to Pamlico Point to hunt ducks, I got hit in the head and knocked out by a flying decoy anchor in the dark. That was the last straw. If, in a weak moment, I succumb to the temptation to go off on another boondoggle, I have instructed my wife to hit me in the head with a hammer. This would achieve basically the same effect without spending any money; getting cold and wet in the rain, ice and snow or getting lost or skunked. ↓↓

Big John Hislop and the author display their Alabama longbeards dispatched at Cullum Walker's Quail Crossing Plantation and Health Spa for old farts.

Cullum invited the fellows to come down and hunt, hoping that they would take care of the meanest and oldest turkey on the farm, Old Moses.

Instead, the author shot a 24-pound gobbler, the biggest one ever shot on the farm. Big John bumped off a 21-pound bird on the same day. Their story follows in the next chapter.

CHAPTER TEN

"Alabama Here I Come"
There is no such thing
as an overdose of turkey hunting.

The best part of turkey hunting, besides dispatching trophy longbeards and sharing the stories, is having hunting buddies scattered all over the country. Turkey hunters are a rare breed, an extraordinary fraternity and a precious fellowship. I have quail-hunting friends. Pheasant hunting friends. A few duck-hunting buddies still. But, my turkey hunting buddies are the crème de la crème. I have found that turkey hunters bond quickly and there is something about turkey hunting that brings out the best in people. They are the blue-collar, red-necked guys, north and south, east and west, who pursue the blue-collar, red-necked and white-headed wild turkey.

The turkey hunters that I know well, whom I call friends, are a humble lot. They are highly skilled, totally dedicated and have dispatched more than their share of birds but you would never know it from their demeanor. You will find no swagger or bravado or braggadocio. For every trophy bird they have brought home, there have been missed shots and botched opportunities. And, they are quite happy to pass a tough bird on to the next hunter.

Take the time, Art killed the Hall Road gobbler. Every hunter in the county went after that tough old bird but Art got it in the end. They were happy to pass that bird on to Art and just as happy that he dispatched it. That is what I am talking about. How many deer hunters do you know that would pass on a monster buck to another hunter? Zero. And I should mention the time Hermit Dave and I passed the Heartbreaker to Art. Boy, is that another great misadventure!

If ever there was a salt of the earth wild bird it is the turkey. The turkey has to work for a living. It sleeps in the trees at night, flies down in the morning and spends the whole day working – looking for food and eating. As the old Bee Gees song goes "staying alive, staying alive." When the sun goes down, it flies back up in the tree and goes to sleep. Day in and day out, it follows the same routine. Wind, rain, snow, cold, ice, tornadoes, it does not matter. Unlike like the US

Mail and the guys in brown, the wild turkey delivers every day, 24-7. It only gets a vacation in the spring, when the gobbler forgets about eating and gets horny. The rest of the time it is work, work, work. This is true wherever you find wild turkeys.

You might find a lazy bird every now and then but don't let that fool you. Jack Robertson, who lives in Springfield, Illinois, had turkeys visiting his house in the late winter. Jack has some great videotape of the birds on the patio, looking into the house. This adds a whole new dimension to the term "peeping tom."

One particular peeping tom of dubious intelligence kept trying to fight its image, which was reflected in the sliding glass doors. Art Kibbe's brother, Knute, had turkeys eating in his backyard another winter. We are talking 10-15 great big gobblers. Knute would feed them out of his hands. Again, another great videotape.

And, lest I forget, Art and Bess had birds visiting their front porch one winter to eat the wild birdseed. During the winter when food is scarce, turkeys will tame up a little and act unafraid. But, come spring in all three cases, the birds disappeared, returned to the wild and back to full-time work.

As I mentioned in the beginning, I have wonderful hunting buddies all over the states and I have been privileged to hunt with all of them on various and sundry occasions. I have not made it to Arizona and New Mexico to hunt with Mark,

143

William and Uncle Bill Crum yet but they are on the itinerary.

I told my wife that after I retire I would start turkey hunting on March 15 and not stop until May 31. I would travel down south first, then the Midwest and finish up in the northeast. I remember reading an article I think that was written by Jerome Robinson. I could be mistaken.

He basically wrote that the first spring after he retired he hunted turkeys for two months non-stop. He hunted all over the country. The purpose of this extended trip was to "get turkey hunting out of his system." He figured he would hunt, hunt and hunt some more until he was absolutely sick to death of turkey hunting. And when he got home he would not want to hunt turkeys anymore.

Au contraire. He had a great adventure and met many new friends. He could not wait to go again! I have shared this story with my wife. She has been forewarned. There is no such thing as an overdose of turkey hunting.

At any rate, one of my dreams was to go to Alabama and hunt turkeys. Before I joined the Steven King Hunt Club – the gang whose eyes glowed in the dark and slobber dripped down their chins - in Cass County, Illinois, I had decided I would save up my money during the off season each year. I would splurge each spring with a visit to the Deep South and start the season early.

I figured I would visit one of those fancy, highfalutin lodges that are advertised in the back of outdoors magazines or seen on TV. The YO Ranch, the King Ranch, Westervelt Lodge, Fisheating Creek Hunt Club, some such destination as that. Deluxe resorts with classy accommodations that charge big bucks for their hunts. High cotton hunt clubs and outfitters where the TV hunters go to videotape their programs, dine on haute cuisine and sip champagne.

Speaking of TV hunters, have you ever noticed that they hunt at these lodges all the time? Or is it just me? In the early days of *Turkey Call TV*, Rob Keck hunted with my buddy, Jack Robertson, at Jack's farm. Nothing fancy there. Been there, seen it. Just another farm in Cass County down the road from our farm. Rob probably stayed at the Motel Six in Beardstown with the Mexicans that work at the hog-processing plant. That part did not make the show. They call that "editing."

You will have to forgive me for poking fun at the TV stars. I know a few and once stayed with them while they were filming in Missouri. They work hard and long hours to get the "film in the can." You could not pay me enough money to work that hard. I have too much fun turkey hunting with my buddies and by myself closer to home. If turkey hunting ever became work, I would quit! Anyhow, back to Alabama.

When we moved back home to North Carolina, I timed it perfectly. The youngest kid had left home for college and the turkey populations in our neck of the woods were increasing. Back-to-back home runs.

Best of all, I met Big John Hislop, from Hubert, N.C., who just happened to belong to my fraternity – Gobble Yelp Gobble - ΓΨΓ. He enjoyed turkey hunting almost as much as I did. I could tell because he told some great stories. John and I chased wild turkeys close to home my first spring season back.

On opening day, I called in two jakes right off the bat at Mr. Herring's farm. We decided to hold off for a larger bird that was lurking in the edge of the woods. It refused to come close so we ended up not getting a bird that day. We hunted several more mornings that season without any luck. I did manage to dispatch a nice gobbler in Chester, South Carolina with Walt Whitman the Father and Walt Whitman the Son. Otherwise known as the two Walts.

I also chased some gobblers at my cousin's farm in Yadkin County with Doc Lucky. Close but no cigar. Cousin Eleanor's country breakfast caused me to miss a big gobbler one morning and I will write that story another day. I passed up on several more shots at jakes around here in Pender County.

One morning late season Big Doug and I kayaked up a creek and got into a mess of gobbling birds but we did not get a clear shot. All in all, I had plenty of fun learning the lay of the land and the habits of eastern North Carolina turkeys. Otherwise known as swamp daddies.

During that first season, John shared stories about hunting in Alabama and he promised to take me there to hunt with his good friend, Cullum Walker, at the Quail Crossing Plantation and Old Folks Health Spa near Clanton. The next spring, John made good on that promise and we headed to Alabama on Easter Monday.

Clanton is a famous landmark in the state. It is south of Birmingham about one hour or so. You can't miss it. Look for the giant peach. There is a huge water tower painted like a peach at the Interstate 65 exit. Actually it looks more like a human body part, a posterior part, than a peach. But it is suppose to be a giant peach. Go figure.

Perhaps you have seen this Alabama wonder in your travels? Perhaps you have even purchased a giant peach T-shirt at the truck stop there? I offered to buy one for John as a thank-you gift for the trip but he preferred a Giant Slurpee instead.

So, after you tear yourself away from the truck stop and the rectum-looking giant peach towering in the azure blue Alabama sky, you head east and before long you reach the private road to Cullum's farm. Which John missed on the first pass. We turned around and found the road on the second pass.

At this point, I was beginning to think boondoggle but we had left Uncle Doug and Hermit Dave at home. We followed the winding gravel road deeper into the woods and countryside. Finally, we reached the gate to the farm and it was unlocked. So far, so good.

When we arrived at the farm, we discovered that we would stay in the guesthouse, which is a lovely restored cabin right out of *Better Homes and Garden* magazine. We're talking heart-pine floors, bedrooms with glass doors that open onto a wrap-around porch, classic stone fireplace, scenic vistas, indoor plumbing and hot running water. The works.

Compared to what I was used to staying in - Tony Knight's farmhouse and the cinder-block bunkhouse at Rose Brook in Missouri - Cullum's country retreat was up-town, high-cotton and almost too swanky for the likes of me. I was used to sleeping on the floor at Tony's, at Rose Brook and at Steele's Motel in McArthur, home of the sagging beds.

But my very own bathroom? And porch? Rocking chairs. Mint juleps. Fresh towels. Mini-bar. Beer-can chicken roasting on the grill. Holy Cow! I could get spoiled hunting at Quail Crossing.

Cullum arrived later for supper and we had a grand time getting acquainted. It turned out that we knew a lot of the same people. Cullum's wife was from Decatur, where I had lived for several years in the early 1950s. Some of my happiest years. Back then, Dad was a research chemist for Monsanto-ChemStran. Small world. Only two degrees of separation between us.

Best of all, Cullum belonged to the same fraternity, ΓΨΓ, shared some great turkey hunting stories and had a bunch of birds on his farm waiting for us in the morning. We feasted on the chicken and other fixings, watched some TV to catch up on news from Iraq – our oldest son was there and in the thick of things at that time - and then headed for bed to get a good night's rest.

I woke up the next morning, five minutes before the alarm went off, went to the kitchen, got the coffee started, stoked up the wood fire to knock the chill off and headed back to my room to dress. So far, so good. No signs of the dreaded boondoggle, yet.

We got dressed, geared up, left the luxury cabin and headed for a remote part of the farm. Once we arrived there we quietly left the truck and cautiously approached a line of trees bordering a large field and food plot. Cullum pointed and whispered that there were birds roosting in the trees. I offered to owl hoot and he said OK.

I proceeded to give out a hoot and three birds gobbled back. A good sign. I need to mention that the weather was excellent, too. A clear, cool morning with stars in the sky. No rain in the forecast. Could that be because I had left

Uncle Doug and Hermit Dave behind? Probably. We closed the distance with John and me setting up on the edge of the tree line and Cullum heading west into another chunk of woods.

Before long the gobblers cranked up and we had three birds within calling distance. We sat quietly and waited until it was time to softly tree call a couple of times. Which I did. The birds flew down about 10 minutes before sunrise. There were gobblers and hens, which is not a good situation but we sat tight and waited.

The closest and loudest gobbler flew down after three or four hens were on the ground. I tried my best to work this bird and get it to come close enough for a shot but we would discover later that it, along with the hens, flew down and landed on the other side of a creek. Thus, calling was useless in this situation.

After it became evident that the birds were gone, we got up and slipped through the woods to the dirt road that paralleled the creek. We followed the road apiece then cut into the woods and set up again. I called periodically on my slate and mouth calls but nothing responded.

After about 30 minutes, John and I got up again and started to troll for birds. We slipped quietly up a hill in front of us and upon reaching the top. *Whuup! Whuup! Whuup!* A gobbler exploded skyward and flew away. After all these years I have not lost my touch in bumping birds. If we had stayed where we sat down in the first place, the bird might have arrived unannounced in the second place. You never know for sure. One thing we did know was it was long gone now.

At any rate, we used the rest of the morning to check the place out and get familiar with this part of the farm. We found Cullum and shared what had happened. He had worked a bird too but no shot. Then he took us to Old Moses' Knob, the home of the oldest, meanest, most cantankerous gobbler on the premises.

There he shared more stories of the duels that occurred between Old Moses and Cullum and other turkey hunting guests. At this point, the score was Old Moses – 100 and Hunters – 0. Naturally, in the spirit of Gobble Yelp Gobble, Cullum was anxious to pass this tough bird on to John or me. We said we were flattered and honored with this gift but would have to think about it.

We headed back to the cabin for lunch, to check the events in Iraq on TV and a short nap. Then we returned to the scene of the crime for the afternoon hunt. John and I passed on Old Moses. I settled for a ground blind on the food plot. John crossed the creek and set up on the edge of a field. After I got situated in the blind, I realized I had left my book back in my room. I would have a hard time staying awake without the book to read.

About every 15 minutes or so, I would run a series of calls on my slate or with my mouth call. Then I would just sit there and nod off to sleep. My eyes would close but my ears would stay open.

About 10 minutes after I had run my fifth or sixth series of calls, I thought I heard a gobble behind me. I was not 100 percent sure since I was slightly napping at the time and contemplated the possibility I could have been dreaming. Nevertheless, I perked up and ran another series of calls and got ready. A few minutes later a gobbler quietly appeared in the corner of the field to my left. Obviously I was not dreaming.

I slowly raised the Eliminator, aimed and squeezed off a round. The bird collapsed on the spot. I left the blind and walked over to retrieve the turkey. A 30-yard shot. It was a dandy. Inch and a quarter spurs. Ten-inch beard. When we weighed it back at the house, it weighed 24 pounds. Cullum remarked that it was the biggest bird ever taken on the farm. Another Holy Cow!

Furthermore, John had been lucky that afternoon as well. He had dispatched a dandy longbeard from across the creek. It was hanging from the porch rafter when we arrived. It weighed a hefty 21 pounds with trophy beard and spurs. Since I had left the Turkey Coffin at home, we put both birds in Cullum's freezer to be mounted by a local taxidermist.

Today, Big Bama Daddy stands at attention atop my bookcase and looks down on the folks who stop by to visit and scrutinize the dead turkeys in my den. It is a big bird and rivals my Missouri, Illinois and North Carolina trophies.

John and I hunted for a couple more days at the farm then left for North Carolina. I did manage to tangle with Old Moses towards the end. I could not resist the challenge. And I came pretty darn close to killing it.

I proceeded to call it in and another gobbler from a nearby hilltop. They got into a fight and forgot all about me. It was a good thing, in retrospect, that I did not dispatch Old Moses. It was enough reward just to hunt in the great state of Alabama, my second home, and get to know Cullum. To shoot the biggest turkey on the farm was icing on the cake. If I had shot Old Moses, too, I would have become *persona non-gratis* and forget about be invited to return.

Cullum reported that somebody finally shot Old Moses the next season. Old Moses' tombstone reads: Old Moses – 101 and Hunter – 1.

I did not return to Alabama last spring to hunt at Quail Crossing. I traveled to Texas instead to hunt with my son, who had safely returned from a year of duty in Iraq. I did not dispatch a Rio on that trip. The Texas weather was cold and windy and the birds did not cooperate much the first week of the season. Very few hunters shot birds, mostly jakes.

I returned home with a sinus and ear infection. My son, the Major select, however dispatched a 21-pound trophy tom a couple of days after I had left. This gobbler turned out to be the biggest one shot on Fort Hood. The apple does not fall far from the turkey-hunting tree. ↓↓

CHAPTER ELEVEN

"The Butter Bar Turkey"
Son Shoots First Turkey

You've got your butterball turkeys from the Piggly Wiggly grocery store. And you've got your "butter bar" gobblers from the Whitman's old hunt club near Chester, South Carolina.

Some kids are lucky and shoot their first turkey when they are young. Say six or seven, maybe 10-12 years old. So young that I wonder if they really appreciate the gift they have been given. You hear about them from your friends or even see them on TV shows. On the other hand, my oldest son shot his first turkey at the ripe old age of 22. And he was old enough to appreciate the gift.

At the time, he was a "butter bar." A second lieutenant in the Army stationed at Ft.

Stewart, Third ID. It was partly my fault that it took so long for him to shoot a turkey. When he was younger and went turkey hunting with me I did not know what the heck I was doing. I did not know a wing beat from a heartbeat.

But, he was to blame too. Varsity Baseball. It was almost impossible for a high school all-conference catcher to miss a baseball game. He made the varsity team as a freshman and played all four years. Since baseball season and spring turkey season just happen to coincide, we had only one occasion to hunt together in four years. That was when he dislocated his thumb and I made a deal with the coach for him to get some medical leave.

The price was easy to pay – a pheasant hunt with the coach at one of my super secret hotspots. We did come close to shooting a turkey the first morning together. I miraculously called a gobbler in but I did not have a clear shot and Heath was out of range.

After high school, there were four years at the Citadel for Heath. His mother and I advised him not to attend this school because they would cut his hair off and yell at him all the time. We bought him a plane ticket and sent him down there for a weekend to visit. When he returned he proudly informed us that he was going to the Citadel. Alas, he did. They cut all his hair off and turned him into a "knob." They yelled at him from the first day that he arrived until a year later, when they recognized him as a third class cadet. We had told him so.

As a reward for surviving his first year at school, I drove down to Charleston, picked him up and we headed for western New York to turkey hunt with Art. Two years had elapsed since his medical leave from baseball to turkey hunt. We had hunted plenty of pheasants and quail during his school breaks, but no turkeys. I figured a trip to New York would be a real treat and it was.

We had a great time with Art and located several leftover gobblers to hunt. While we were there, I made a 50-yard shot on a big tom off Sager Road. The plan was for Heath to shoot it but he was in the wrong spot. The bird passed on my left and Heath was on my right. This would turn out to be a harbinger for future turkey hunts. It would become my destiny to shoot more turkeys even though the plan would call for Heath to shoot them.

Heath and I had roosted the birds in the woods off Sager Road the evening before, so we headed over to them early the next morning. We slipped into the woods where they were asleep in the trees and put out one of those newfangled decoys. Back in those days, Art did not approve of using decoys. He practiced the artistry of calling in a turkey without visual aids. He figured if a bird would not come to your calling then the bird deserved to live another day. If the tom hung up and did not arrive, he would wait awhile then pick up and go somewhere else. Truck time.

At any rate, I had borrowed the decoy from Dan, Art's son. After we got settled in the woods, I crawled about 10 yards out and staked this sucker into the ground. It was a brand new Feather Flex decoy, the only ones at that time for sale, and it would not expand from its folded position. So, I blew into the hole in the bottom where the stake goes.

Now, I was doing this in the dark and could not see very well. The next thing I heard was a loud *pop!* I had blown the decoy up! I had blown so hard that the silly thing split wide open at the seam. Boy, did I feel stupid. Anyway, I recovered quickly and staked the decoy into the ground. I bought Dan a new decoy later.

The exploded decoy did not make much difference. The birds flew down and went the other way. We sat there for awhile since Art was in charge of the operation. Finally, he realized we were left high and dry. So he suggested we follow the birds and find out where they went. I told him that I figured the birds had headed for the old cornfield where we had seen them hanging around the day before.

But, he thought they had gone to a different location. So, we headed through the woods to his spot first. Upon arrival we discovered that it was empty. We then made our way to the cornfield and sneaked up to the edge.

Lo and behold, the small flock of turkeys were in the field. Three hens were slowly walking along and picking the ground for seeds and old corn. The gobbler, which was a big'un, was strutting its stuff as hard as it could. Out in the adjacent field, Art could see a jake.

We proceeded to quietly spread out along the edge of the field and hunker down. Art, then me 10 yards to the right, then Heath another 10 yards over. It did not take Art's calling long to coax the hens out of the field and into the woods towards him. It did take the old gobbler a few minutes to realize the hens had left and it proceeded to depart the field and catch up to the hens. During its departure, the tom made a fatal error. It stopped in the corner of the field and strutted one last time.

Kablam! My Winchester 1300 dropped it dead in its tracks. I shot through an opening about the size of a basketball between two bushes. I figured it was a 40-yard shot. So, when the tom finished strutting its stuff and stepped into the opening, I squeezed off a round and it fell over dead. Art arrived and paced off the shot.

According to Art's measurements, it was 50 yards. I apologized to Heath for shooting "his" turkey but he understood the situation and the fact that he just did not have a shot. I promised to find another turkey that evening and make up for what had happened. And I did.

The next morning we set up on Hodge Gulf over at Al Brown's farm, where I had roosted a bird the evening before. I left my shotgun in the truck and carried the video camera. We set up across the gulf from the bird and Art proceeded to call it in.

When it arrived, I had the camera shot but Heath did not have a clear shot with the gun. The tom lingered for the camera then departed up the gulf. We chased after it for awhile but could never coax it back. It was our last morning to hunt and we went home without him dispatching a turkey. We still had a great time together and figured one way or another we would hunt again.

While at the Citadel, Heath met Walt Whitman the Son. They were in Alpha Company and would become fast and close friends from that day forward. Walt loved to turkey hunt and lived in Chester, South Carolina. Walt's parents, Walt the Father and Ruth, adopted Heath as their second son and Walt and Heath chased turkeys in Chester when the school would give them leave. If memory serves me, Walt the Son shot his first turkey during those three years but Heath did not. He missed a couple and even got lost in the woods a time or two, so we heard later.

This is a good place to mention, that not only did Heath get a second family in South Carolina but so did we. We adopted the Whitmans and vice versa. We have been close friends for many, many years. Walt the Father and I have hunted turkeys and fly-fished for trout almost every year since those early Citadel days. I also should add that Heath met his future wife there thanks to Walt the Son, who arranged a blind date with a certain Southern belle named, Heather Wiley. All roads seem to lead to Chester.

After graduation, Heath was commissioned a second lieutenant in the Army, went to OBC at Fort Knox, became an armor officer in the 369 and was posted at Ft. Stewart in Savannah, Georgia. The following spring on Easter weekend, he got leave to hunt turkeys in Chester. I flew out from St. Louis on Easter Sunday afternoon and the boys picked me up in Charlotte. They were late arriving at the airport but they had a good excuse. They had roosted birds in a creek bottom on Walt's hunt club.

I had arrived too late to buy a South Carolina hunting license, which looking back, was a good thing. I would do the turkey calling and not the shooting. Thus, I would not shoot another bird meant for Heath. A brilliant stroke of planning! We headed back to Chester and spent the night with Walt and Ruth. And Punkin.

Punkin was their pet beagle that went to the pantry door and barked when she wanted dog biscuits. She went often. The next morning we awoke and departed for the hunt club. Big Walt went along too. A double father-son hunt.

Ordinarily, when four people turkey hunt together it is a formula for failure. Turkey hunters are like hunting dogs. One dog is enough, is manageable and does the trick. You have two dogs and your troubles triple, not double, but triple. You have four dogs and your troubles increase at an exponential rate similar to Pi. When four people hunt turkeys together your chance for failure is a sure bet. We're talking Titanic and the iceberg bet.

About the only way to make it work is to cross your fingers, pray and strike bargains with the devil. On the other hand, two fathers and two sons were worth the trouble. Just maybe things would work out.

It took about 30 minutes to drive from town out to a large tract of paper company land that several hunters in North and South Carolina leased for turkey and deer hunting. We parked our vehicle and the boys led the old men down the path through the forest to the creek bottom and the turkeys. We slipped into the bottom quietly and found good trees to sit against. It was still dark and we had managed to not bump any birds out of the trees so far.

No sooner did we get situated did I get the urge to purge. It never fails. Essence of woods is a marvelous laxative that even the most constipated can not resist. I whispered to my son, who was sitting next to me and beginning to suspect something was up, that I had to excuse myself for a couple of minutes. He understood since he too sometimes suffered from the same malady. Usually when duck hunting.

I was able to crawl quietly and in between colon spasms down into the ditch beside the creek and locate a suitable leaner tree. I quickly took care of business without making much noise or soiling my pants or suspenders. My son had supplied me with an ample amount of government-issue striking paper, which I put to good use. The next trick was to climb out of the ditch and back to the tree without making any noise or bump any turkeys. As I have shared before, I was an expert at bumping turkeys.

Miraculously, I returned to the tree and sat down beside my son without any disturbance or disorder. Then we waited for the woods to become lighter and the turkeys to wake up. They proceeded to do so. And that is when we noticed that there were hens roosting in the trees between the gobblers and us. That was not a good thing I whispered to my son. The presence of hens meant we had to compete with the real deal. The hens would fly down and more than likely lead the gobblers away. Been there, seen that, too many times.

Before long we heard soft tree calls and young Walt and I joined the conversation with our own calling. We were close enough to watch the turkeys in the trees and gauge their reaction to our soft yelps. So far, so good. Finally, the hens flew down first and landed across the creek to our right. Next, two jakes flew down and landed with the hens.

If there was a longbeard or two present, we did not see them fly down. They were probably a tad farther up the creek and out of sight. After the birds that we could see landed, I began to call to them with excited yelps and cutts. Soon, the hens appeared and eventually walked by on the other side of the creek and out of the picture. The situation was improving. Perhaps, the gobblers would soon appear.

Next came the two jakes. But since they could not see the hens anymore, they hopped over the small creek and climbed the bank in front of Heath and me and headed for my calling. A couple of minutes later, they appeared in front of us only 25 yards away. Heath had his shotgun on one of them so I whispered, "Shoot." And he did. The bird flipped over dead. The other jake ran off to our left and right into young Walt's gun range. *Kablam!* And it was almost dead. It flopped and ran several more yards into the woods then expired.

We retrieved both birds and headed back to the truck for a coffee break and a chance to let the events sink in. Heath had finally dispatched a turkey, albeit a jake. But it did not matter to us. We were lucky, extremely fortuitous to be able to hunt that morning period. Heath had to report back to duty the next day. He did not have more time to stay and hunt. That Easter Monday morning was it. This time things turned out well. Hunters – 2 and Turkeys – 0.

We headed back to town so the boys could clean their turkeys and Big Walt and I could go buy me a license. After Heath had finished with his bird, he packed up and headed back to Ft. Stewart. The two Walts and I would hunt together for the next several days. During the course of those days, we manage to locate lots of turkeys and shoot none. I missed a bird one morning with Big Walt. Shot under it and hit a log instead. I was using a borrowed shotgun and figured later that it shot low.

Walt the Father also missed a bird that I called in. It was a tad out of range – I am being nice here. We also tried on several mornings to work birds that we later discovered were being fed by the neighboring hunt club. It is darn difficult to call birds in when they are being baited to go elsewhere. The game warden was promptly informed and took care of the situation.

Since that "butter bar" hunt many years ago, the Whitman's and I have shared many more hunts together. We have missed shots at more turkeys and we have dispatched some nice longbeards, too. To the best of my memory, and I may be mistaken, the Army and Saddam Hussein have kept my son from joining us in South Carolina to turkey hunt since that Easter Monday long ago. Our plans for the following spring season got cancelled when Heath's brigade was sent to Kuwait during Desert Thunder.

To keep the morale up, I created my legendary *Tailfeathers* newsletter and mailed it to the soldiers who manned their tanks on the Iraq border. It would be three years later, after his promotion to Captain and while he was at Ft. Knox, that Heath and I would hunt together again. I included that story in an earlier chapter. And, I just happened to shoot "his" turkey again.

I have a son-in-law, Brock, and he has shot his first turkey. I called it in for him and he dispatched it out at the Upper 125 farm in Cass County. I had my gun with me but I resisted the temptation to shoot it. The stakes were high. He was about to marry my daughter at the time and I did not want to piss him off. Thus, he shot the longbeard that I was saving later for me. One more sacrifice for my daughter.

I have a younger son, Ian, who hunts turkeys too. He is not in the Army. He is a senior in college, but is just as busy as his older brother was, going to school and working part-time. He has yet to shoot a turkey. He has had many chances and has missed several birds. It is partly my fault because I was learning to hunt new terrain in Illinois.

Howsumever, he is partly to blame, too. Baseball. Again. Ian played all four years in high school. He was a pitcher, outfielder and infielder. He suffered no serious injuries during the regular seasons. Thus, no medical leave for hunting turkeys. He did break his nose during a practice for the state tournament. But that was during the summer. Perhaps, if he had been a catcher like his older brother, things would have been different?

Ian is 22 years old. Maybe this spring will be his lucky season. He is old enough to appreciate the gift of dispatching a wild turkey. If only I could talk him out of fly-fishing long enough to shoot one. A trip to western New York

166

after college graduation might just do the trick. I
will leave my shotgun at home. I promise. ↓↓

CHAPTER TWELVE

"Weird Turkeys"
Professor Privette Pontificates

F riends, having duly graduated from that fine and esteemed institution, Pascagoula University of Taxidermy and Turkeyology, P.U.T.T. for short, I am imminently qualified to pontificate, prevaricate and postulate on the various and sundry turkey deviations, derivations and deputations that occur in the natural order of selection. I now hold a T.D. in epidemiological Turkeyology, Summa cum Dental Epidermal, and therefore have become a bone fide expert in the field. Not just a good amateur. You may address me as Dr. Privette or Professor or plain, "Hey You!" Eat your heart out James Earl Kennamer. You have met your match!

A couple of cosmological events convinced me to seek and thus attain this lofty degree. One, I had read all the books in existence on turkey hunting and had come to the conclusion that 99 percent of the context was manure, fodder and fire kindling. The one percent of decent material belonged to Tom Kelly and Lovett Williams.

Second, I happened to pick up a matchbook at the Full Strut Bar and Grill and on the back cover was an advertisement for PUTT and it various degree programs. Since I was not interested in nasal proctology, advanced greens keeping, philatelist technician or rotor-rooter specialist, I checked the remaining square for more information on the science of turkeyology.

One thing led to another and the butt bone is connected to the head bone, forsooth, after ten long years of burning the midnight oil I finally received the post graduate degree aforementioned above via long distance and telekinetic correspondence.

The following discourse is a summary of my doctoral dissertation. I hope you enjoy it. The people at PUTT did and have nominated me for their Turkey Hall of Fame.

Forsooth, have you ever noticed that no two turkeys are exactly alike? I have six stuffed examples residing in my turkey den and they are all very different. Not just in weight – they all weigh more than 21 pounds. But they all have strange features. For example, not all of my turkeys have matching spurs. You would think that spurs, like earrings, should match. (We do not count ones that have broken off.) But they don't. The Swamp Daddy has one spur that is two inches long, sharp and curved. The other spur is about one-inch long and no sign of break off. The spurs do not match. Thus, I have duly christened this anomaly as *spurious deviatus e pluribus unum*.

I have another bird that only has one spur period. There is no spur on the other leg nor is there any evidence of there ever being a spur on that leg. The truth is that several turkeys I have bumped off over the years have had strange spurs or lack thereof. I remember shooting one turkey, a longbeard, and it did not have any spurs. And I have friends who have killed birds that had multiple spurs and strange-looking spurs. I have named this condition *pernicious spurious absentious et variosis*.

And, then there is the obvious weird beard situation. Some of my birds had multiple beards. No big deal. Some of them had short beards, broken off by ice, snow, mites, fungus or the beard-eating fairy? You tell me because nobody seems to know for sure what makes a beard break off or stop growing or whatever? At this point I have heard so much crapola that I am leaning towards the fairy theory, otherwise known as *beardus minimus fariosis woodensis*. And I anxiously await proof otherwise.

I remember one particular spring in New York, a lot of hunters brought in birds with super short beards, stubby things with brown stain on the ends of the fibers. Art's son, Dan, from Reno shot one of them. I got there later in the season and shot another one. These were mature birds with long spurs and short jake-like beards. A definite case of *beardus minimus whateverus.*

Another spring season, Art shot a nice tom near his Cousin Bill's place. I was with him at the time. The gobbler had horrible looking feet. Deformed feet. We called them Fu Manchu feet. The feet were all bent up and crooked with super long sharp toenails. Killer toenails. Scary looking feet. We experts call that *scariosis fu manchuvious pedimentus semper fidelis.*

That same spring, Scott Forbes, Art's nephew, shot a gobbler and when he went to pick it up all the tail feathers fell out. That was one weird looking bird. A tail-less turkey. I got a picture of it around here somewhere. It ain't pretty. I suspect after further scrutiny, study and cogitation that the turkey suffered from a severe case of ass pucker.

The resultant physiological response, the sudden loss of tail feathers, was caused by the rectumnal muscles contracting at the speed of light and triggering the opposite response in the body part known as the *popeus noseus*. Hence, we have titled this condition in honor of Scott – *Forbeous rectumous posteriorus absentus.* In short, the Forbes ass-pucker syndrome.

Again, while hunting in New York, rumor had it that hunters had seen a white wild turkey.

I have studied pictures of white wild turkeys and they were not pure white. Lovett Williams called it a "smoke gray appearance" and the birds in the pictures were grayish white or whitish gray? Take your pick. But they were not pure white like their butterball cousins cooped up in the turkey pens. Anyhow, I did not meet or talk to anyone who actually saw the New York white turkey. Art said that he doubted the veracity of the source. A hunter named Polk.

Forsooth, I, on the other hand, while pursuing my post graduate degree, have seen a white turkey in the wild. Not one white turkey but several and on numerous occasions. And to back up my truthfulness I have actual videotape footage of these white turkeys along side their brethren and sistren dark brown turkeys. There may even be a Sasquatch in the background of one of the tapes. Can't tell for sure. But the tapes do not lie and sell for $29.95.

We have white wild turkeys in eastern North Carolina. Specifically in Onslow County and along the White Oak River. Come on down and I will show you. The complete tour package, including a hotdog and drink from Paul's Place, costs $39.95.

I spotted my first white turkey while riding the county roads with Big John Hislop a few years back. We were pre-season scouting and keeping track of the number of birds and their locations. We were just up the road from Stella when we spotted a white dot amongst the black dots in the back of a large field. John pulled the truck over and we watched the birds through our binoculars. Sure enough, there was a white bird in the thick of the flock. We saw this particular bird on several more occasions.

The next spring I was riding the road again by myself but with my video camera. This time I encountered another white turkey mixed in with the regular turkeys in a sod field right up next to the highway. I pulled over and captured some great close-up shots of the birds. This particular white bird turned out to be a gobbler and did some strutting. On up the road at a distant cousin's farm, I watched two more white gobblers and one hybird bird participate in flock follies.

This past spring Big Doug and I were preseason scouting in the woods. We found lots of fresh scratch in an area that held birds every year. Then we heard wing beats and Doug said he saw a white turkey fly up from the brush. He was sober at the time. Later on during the hunting season, I called in a white Jake while hunting in that vicinity. I got a very good look at this bird while I sat in my blind and it loafed within five yards of me. A very good look down the length of my shotgun barrel.

The bird carried a wild bird frame, long, lean, no oversized farm bird head or butterball breast. Its beard was about 5 inches long and as black as coal. The rest of its feathers were white, white as a tame duck's. This turkey acted wild. Looked wild. But its feathers screamed tame turkey. Again weird. Well, I sat there in my blind wondering if I should shoot this bird or not. I figured it would be my misfortune to shoot it and then get accused of killing some farmer's tame turkey. But, if I shot it, I could examine it and maybe get the wildlife people to check it out and solve the mystery once and for all.

I thought about it for awhile and decided not to shoot. I chose to keep the mystery alive and avoid all the crap from my buddies. Plus, a larger normal colored longbeard arrived later and now it is stuffed and standing on my coffee table.

Maybe one of these days I will meet up with a wildlife biologist and ask her what the heck is going on with the white wild turkeys. To my knowledge there are no poultry farms in the part of the county where I keep seeing the white birds. Lots of hog farms. But no turkey farms. This sort of removes the theory of an escaped tame turkey from the formula. Somebody could have released a couple of farm birds but why?

Another source reported that my distant cousin, Jim, or his son, shot one of the white turkeys but I have not talked to them lately to find out if it was true. Hence, for the time being, we will identify this white characteristic as the *whitosis turkeosis whitosis oakus* or plain white turkey for short.

Then there was that hermit gobbler that Hermit Dave shot a long time ago. Dave said the bird had a super long beard, extra long spurs and moss growing on its head, but it weighed less than 16 pounds. This in Dave's terminology actually translates to 12 pounds. Now that is one skinny ass bird. Since hermit gobblers do not result from genetic or biologic root causes, standard epidemiology, we will refer this situation to the idiot pet doctor on the radio. Dr. What's-His-Name? The one who loves cats?

I happened to listen to this idiot pet doctor on the radio one afternoon in my workshop. The tuning knob broke and I was stuck with Doctor Crap-For-Brains. A lady, with a whiny-ass voice, called into his show and complained that her pet cat was peeing all over the house. You should have heard the long-winded, complicated explanation for this behavior and the darn recommended treatment! Give me a break.

The ancient Egyptians built the pyramids faster and easier than the doctor's recommended treatment for the peeing cat. I was sitting there thinking to heck with all that rigmarole. Give me the darn cat. I will take it on a one-way ride to the Pound. It can pee all it wants and where it wants for two weeks. Then, sweet dreams, pussy! Anyway, back to turkeys.

Dave Chase had a pet gobbler in his backyard for a couple of years. Now it looked normal but it acted weird. It was a watch turkey, a *turkeosis guardatosis hatwhuupupus*, and would run after strangers and attack them. Dave would toss his hat on the ground and the bird would whuup up on it. I think Art has the video of Dave's bird and its antics. Too bad the gobbler died before Dave could get on David Letterman's show and the stupid pet segment. He could have made some money showing that crazy bird off. Again, another referral to the Pet Doctor.

And then there was the mad gobbler in Logan County, Ohio, which is north of Dayton that attacked fly-fishermen on the Mad River. The DNR relocated a bunch of birds in the river valley and one of them kept attacking the fishermen. It got its picture in the paper. And hit on the head several times with fly rods.

People here tell about a gobbler that hung out on Western Boulevard and chased cars, a definite strain of the *turkeosis dogatosis chevroletus*. That was before my time. Before we moved to Jacksonville. I have had enough people tell me about the turkey that I guess it was true.

Again, I must add that these behavioral deviations are best diagnosed by animal psychologists and pet psychics because weird behavior does not always have a basis in physiological, biological or genetic material. A simple explanation would be that neglectful, abusive and/or indulgent parents reared these birds.

Finally, we must not forget to include the bearded hen turkey. A distant but nonetheless ornithological relative of the bearded ladies in the county fairs. You do remember the tent next to the Hoochy Koochy ladies who did remarkable anatomical tricks with Ping-Pong balls? 1968, the Durham County Fair? Thus, hen turkeys are known to exhibit beards and spurs. I have not seen spurred lady turkeys yet because I have limited my harvest of hens to just a few for Thanksgiving dinner. On the other hand, Shawn Gray of Chautauqua County is famous for dispatching bearded hens during the spring season. He is fast becoming an expert and should be consulted if you have any questions. I have his address.

Alas, I reckon I have dissertated enough on this subject. If perchance, you hunt wild turkeys long enough you are bound to run into some strange birds. Genetics, abusive parents, voodoo and global warming probably have a lot to do with the variety of aberrations. But if anybody can set me straight on the short, stubby beards I would appreciate it. Until then I am sticking with my beard-eating woods fairy hypothesis. *Beardus minimus fariosis woodensis.*

Say goodnight, Dr. Bill.

"Goodnight everybody." ↓↓

A Preview From the Next Book

BOHIC – Bend Over Here It Comes!
More Tall Tales, Gibberish, Malarkey &
Balderdash While Hunting Wild Turkeys

"You Snooze, You Lose"
Grandpa Lem's Gobbler

If I had a dollar for every time I fell asleep while hunting turkeys, I would be so rich that I could retire, buy one of those high dollar turkey plantations and hunt it all by myself! Alas, if only. Instead, I have lots of stories about falling asleep and missing turkeys. One of my favorite misadventures featured my cousin Eleanor's cooking. She and her husband live on a farm in Yadkin County, North Carolina and they invited me to visit them and hunt their wild turkeys. I was happy to oblige and squeezed them in last year on my return from western New York.

I broke up a 12-hour trip home by stopping and spending the night with them. Plus, I was able to hunt turkeys the next morning, which was the next-to-last day of the N.C. season. I went to bed early and told my cousin I would get up around 5 a.m. and for her to stay in bed and not worry about me. I would fend for myself. About 15 minutes before the alarm went off, I woke up and smelled breakfast cooking downstairs in the kitchen. I dressed and followed my nose.

Cousin Eleanor had gotten up and was in the kitchen cooking me the finest country breakfast you could imagine. We're talking a feast – country ham, red-eye gravy, home-made biscuits and jelly, scrambled fresh farm eggs, the works! Naturally, I had time to sit down and eat my fill. I chided Eleanor for fixing this fine meal but I was truly grateful. She was supposed to be sleeping, not cooking. But she seemed happy to fix it for me and her cooking reminded me of my own mother's home cooking.

After I finished breakfast, I departed the kitchen and hiked up the hill behind her house. I got about half way up the hill when the essence of woods kicked in. The full stomach did not help the situation. I quickly located a suitable leaner tree and took care of business. Then I readjusted my clothing and headed for the hilltop where I had left a great big gobbler the year before. No sooner, did I sit down and get situated did the bird announce its presence with a hearty gobble. It was roosting in the same darn spot as it had been the year before. We're talking déjà vu all over again.

Well, I perked up and softly tree called a couple of times and waited. I heard the gobbler fly down, a little below me and to the right. I poured it on with excited yelps and cutts and the tom gobbled back profusely. Next, I shut up, raised my gun and waited. Nothing. After a while, the bird gobbled again and it was up the ridge and farther away. I knew where it was headed, to a field next to the creek, but I decided to sit tight and wait for it to return. That was its pattern last year. Besides I had the most comfortable spot I had ever sat in. The tree behind my back fit perfectly. The leaves on the ground underneath my foam pad caressed my butt. I felt great.

Well, before long that big breakfast kicked in and I fell fast asleep. It was inevitable. And while I slept, eyes closed and ears open, I started to dream about that big turkey returning to me and strutting and drumming. The dream was so vivid that I could swear the turkey was right behind me. Holy Cow, it was right behind me! I was not dreaming. While I slept, the big bird crept. Silently it sneaked in behind me and before I could wake up and get my gun on it, it slipped away, back down the hill. This was not the first time I had slept through a gobbler. It would not be the last time either.

Another of my favorite falling asleep stories stars my buddy, Tim Spengler, and his late father, Grandpa Lem. Tim, Lem, Uncle John and I went out to the Cass County farm one morning to hunt turkeys. Tim, Lem and Uncle John had never shot a turkey. So it was my job to help them out. The problem is that four turkey hunters are darn near impossible to maneuver in the woods without making a ruckus and bumping turkeys. I wisely chose to set them up in the brush on the edge of an alfalfa field and I would try to call birds out of the woods and into our gun range.

I sat next to Tim in the middle and the old-timers took the flanks – Uncle John to the left, Grandpa Lem to the right. After we had settled down, I got the urge to nap so I put Tim in charge of watching the field and I would call some and then nap some. Before long, Tim woke me up and informed me that two gobblers had appeared on the other side of the field. I perked up and proceeded to call these birds across the field and almost into gun range.

Mysteriously, the birds, two jakes, abruptly halted at the edge of our range and began to act nervous. I was a bit puzzled at their behavior until out of the corner of my eye I spotted another tom in full strut approaching our set up from the right. It was the boss tom and the other two birds knew to keep their distance.

Tim and I watched the big bird approach and in just a couple of seconds it would be right smack dab in front of Grandpa Lem. Twenty yards out and an easy shot. Just one problem. When we turned to look at Grandpa Lem, he was

sound asleep sitting on his bucket, gun in his lap
... ↓↓↓

Publisher note: This is a tease for the next book, *BOHIC, Bend Over Here It Comes!,* which is scheduled for publication summer 2006.

We will mail out a pre-publication flyer and order blank and offer the same First Edition limited number of copies, signed and numbered, as we did for this book.

We plan on publishing several more turkey hunting books in the future and we will offer each one as a First Edition, special limited number of copies, signed and numbered. After that we will proceed with this general printing and public sales edition.

If you wish to be on our mailing list for First Editions, please send us your name and address at Tailfeather Press, 1119 Hendricks Avenue, Jacksonville, NC 28540. Thanks!

Order Form

Bend Over Shake a Tailfeather
Books and CDs

Tailfeather Press & Taxidermy International
1119 Hendricks Avenue, Jacksonville, NC 28540
Email: frbill@bizec.rr.com

Postal & Phone Orders:

Mail this order form to: Bill Privette-Tailfeather Press, 1119 Hendricks Avenue, Jacksonville, NC 28540. Or phone: 910.455.5713.

Please send: _____ book/s @ $19.95 each **plus shipping** to:

Please send: _____ 80-minute CD/s @ $14.95 each **plus shipping** to:

Name: _____

Address: _____

City: _____

State: _____ Zip Code: _____

Shipping: One book/CD: $3. Two books/CD: $4. Three or more books/CD: $5. Allow seven (7) business days for delivery.

Write checks to Bill Privette. You may return book/s for full refund if you are not satisfied.

Visit our website soon: turkeyhuntbooks.com.